COMPUTER IMAGE GENERATION

COMPUTER IMAGE GENERATION

Edited by

BRUCE J. SCHACHTER

A Wiley-Interscience Publication

John Wiley & Sons

New York   Chichester   Brisbane   Toronto   Singapore

Library of Congress Cataloging in Publication Data
Main entry under title:

Computer image generation.

  "A Wiley-Interscience publication."
  Bibliography: p.
  Includes indexes.
    1. Computer graphics. I. Schachter, Bruce J. (Bruce
Jay), 1946-   .
  T385.C5934   1983   001.64'43   82-17366
  ISBN 0-471-87287-3

Printed in the United States of America

10 9 8 7 6 5 4 3 2 1

PREFACE

The most sophisticated computer graphics systems being used today are computer image generation devices producing video images in real time (30 frames per second). This book provides detailed descriptions of the algorithms and architectures used in all major computer image generation (CIG) devices, and covers other important topics associated with CIG, such as antialiasing, data-base design, the generation of special effects, and future architectures for image generation.

This book is the outgrowth of a substantial research and development effort by the authors over the past several years and is intended to be an immediate resource for anyone working in CIG or considering its uses and future applications. It is also relevant to anyone interested in sophisticated computer graphics presentations, and can be used as a textbook for a second course in computer graphics.

Because of the many recent scientific and technological advances in CIG, the areas in which CIG can be applied are growing rapidly. This book will serve as a reference to the current technological state-of-the-art and as a guide to existing and potential applications. As the performance/price ratio of computer hardware improves, many additional applications of CIG will become feasible. There is enormous potential for the use of CIG in a wide variety of fields, from Hollywood movies, video games, and dance choreography to the programming of robots, traffic simulation, and military training. However, because the most successful application of CIG has been in visual training simulators, much of the book is devoted to discussing them. This information on visual training simulators should be of interest to anyone concerned with other applications of CIG, and it is intended that the discussion will be used by readers as an example and guide to the many other possible uses of CIG.

VISUAL TRAINING SIMULATORS

Visual training simulators present scenes to an observer to allow him or her to practice some task, such as flying an airplane. To start with, a three-dimensional (3-D) model of some area of the world is prepared and stored on magnetic disk. This model is called the visual data base. The visual simulator combines an image generator with an electrooptical display system. The image generator reads-in blocks of 3-D data from magnetic disk and transforms them into 2-D scene descriptions. These 2-D data are then converted to analog video which is presented to the trainee through television monitors (or projectors) and optical components. The generated imagery is meant to be representative of the true scenes that the trainee would see if he or she were performing the actual task being simulated.

Some of the other potential uses of CIG are discussed below. These include applications appropriate to manufacturing, entertainment, medicine, the military, the arts, and sports, just to name a few.

ANIMATION AND MOVIES

While much publicity has surrounded the use of computerized special effects in high budget science fiction movies, thus far little of this has had anything to do with CIG. Most special effects relate to the use of digitally controlled cameras to film miniature models (such as spacecraft), and the hardware used for this has much in common with that used for numerical control of machine tools. Although the recent Walt Disney Productions motion picture TRON (Figure 1) represents a significant step in the development of movies where the image seen on screen is actually generated by computer, except for TRON, computer graphics in any form still has not found much use in the film industry. The situation should change when realistic looking images can be generated in a cheaper, quicker, and easier manner by computer than by artistry or by photographing models, but in the near future, computer graphics will mainly be used for "filling" and "in-betweening" in cartoon animation, and for creating a limited amount of high-priced footage designed to dazzle the viewer (Figure 2b).

The 2-D task of in-betweening (interpolating between key frames drawn by a master animator) is being worked on at a number of places such as the New York Institute of Technology [REEV82]. However, since the 2-D scenes being interpolated are really projections of 3-D scenes in the "mind's eye" of the master animator, this is a difficult task to do properly.

Another task which is now sometimes done by computer is that of

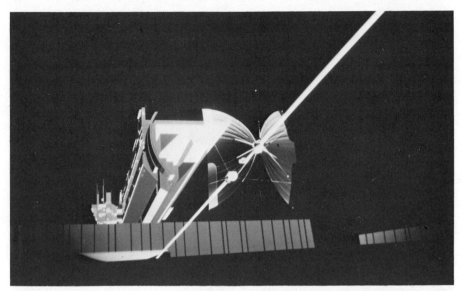

Figure 1.   A scene from the Disney movie TRON, © Walt Disney Productions.

filling in regions of an animator's line drawing [SMIT79]. Colors are allocated to areas displaying the digitized drawing on a TV screen and having the operator point to the areas with a light pen or cursor. Instead of using a camera setup to shoot the finished image, it is automatically sent out to magnetic video disk or tape, or digital film recorder. Animation by artistry is now too expensive for studios to replicate the high quality found in such Disney films as Pinnochio or Fantasia. In order for CIG systems to come into widespread use here, the cost would have to go down considerably, and 3-D data bases would have to be made easier to create and manipulate.

MOTION ANALYSIS

Motion analysis is the study of the movement of humans, animals, organisms, and machines. Motion analysis through real-time or time-lapse photography is a central tool in numerous fields. For example, cardiologists examine the form and movement of the left ventricle of the heart, kinesiologists study the gait of individuals suffering from a variety of disabilities, coaches scrutinize the body movements of athletes to improve their performance, and engineers work out the motions of the articulated parts of a robot manipulator.

Models used in the analysis of motion can also be used in its synthesis.

Figure 2. Images created by Digital Effects, Inc. personnel. (a) Video palette image; © DEI/Mark Lindquist, 1981. (b) Calligraphic landscape; © DEI/Grey Adv. for Timex, 1981. (Photographs used by permission.)

Graphical simulations have been used for years to visualize the move-ments associated with sign language, dance, robot assembly, and vehicu-lar crashes. Badler and Smoliar [BADL79] state:

> *Animation of human movement requires the specification of the body as an object for display and a suitable set of commands which operate on that specification to change its articulated form and position in space. Since we desire data and control structures which will serve as a model of human movement, we cannot use traditional 2-D and 2½-D modeling techniques frequently employed by conventional and computer animators.*

The human body is typically depicted with one of the following ap-proaches. (1) The limbs and joints are abstracted as a stick figure, (2) curved surfaces are used to explicitly depict exterior surfaces, and (3) boolean combinations of volumes are used.

A stick figure is not well-suited for representing occlusions, but is simple to generate. With a simple stick figure it is easy to confuse clock-wise and counterclockwise rotation.

The problems associated with stick figures can be overcome by adding "skin and muscle" to surround the "bones." The body surface can be formed from either curved or planar patches. The difficulty with this approach lies in modeling the regions around flexing joints.

The body can also be decomposed into articulated primitive solids such as spheres, ellipsoids, or cylinders. The general shape of the body can be portrayed well by a small number of ellipsoids.

A real-time visual simulator would be very handy to most persons working in these fields. A choreographer could feed the simulator dance notation and immediately see the dance "performed." An engineer could input a computer tape and then examine the movement of a robot arm or machine tool.

TRAFFIC SIMULATION

Traffic systems are difficult to design due to the complexities of the many space–time interactions. Mathematical models are used for the analysis of alternative configurations under varying conditions. The most detailed analyses are made by simulation. Through computer graphics, the simula-tion can be made visible, allowing the designers to better evaluate system performance. The objective of most current graphic simulations is to achieve a realistic portrayal which reflects the condition of a network at some points in time. A continuous real-time graphic simulation, of course, would facilitate the understanding of system dynamics.

Although traffic engineers have developed considerable skill in the analysis of simple systems, it is still difficult for them to predict the workings of complex linked arrangements. It is necessary that a complex urban configuration allow high utilization and avoid chaos despite wide fluctuations in traffic flow and road conditions. Computer models should ideally incorporate coordinated signaling; route selection, lane change, and queueing statistics; and the effects of road construction, traffic accidents, and weather conditions. A real-time simulation model should allow the engineer to readily vary system parameters and immediately observe results.

COMPUTER AIDED DESIGN/COMPUTER AIDED MANUFACTURING (CAD/CAM)

CAD/CAM systems automate many analysis and drafting operations associated with product design. The heart of the CAD/CAM system is the design terminal or graphic workstation (Figures 3 and 4). The CAD/CAM engineer interacts with the workstation to develop, modify, manipulate, and refine the design by referring to menus on a screen, pointing to screen and tablet positions, responding to system prompts, and typing in data and commands. Once the design is formulated the engineer lets the system make a hard copy or computer tape.

CAD/CAM is becoming the normal way to design and manufacture a product. As a design is developing, the CAD/CAM system is accumulating and storing geometric and character descriptions of every design element. The design process is speeded up since documentation is systematized and the redrafting of commonly used components is simplified. The graphic data base is beginning to replace the paper drawing as the design record. Eventually a data description may be fed directly into an automated factory (possibly via telephone line), and the factory will manufacture a part to its specification.

Storage tubes have been popular in CAD/CAM in the past because of their high resolution, low cost, and lack of flicker. The main problem is that to update the storage tube display, it must first be blanked out (causing it to flash), and then be completely rewritten. Stroke-writing refresh tubes can be updated more quickly, but like storage tubes are best suited for depicting "wire-frame" drawings. In the not-too-distant future, storage

Figure 3. A Calma work station with 3-D graphics being displayed in color. The resolution of the display is 1280 × 1024 pixels. The graphics on the screen depicts the intersection between a cone and cylinder.

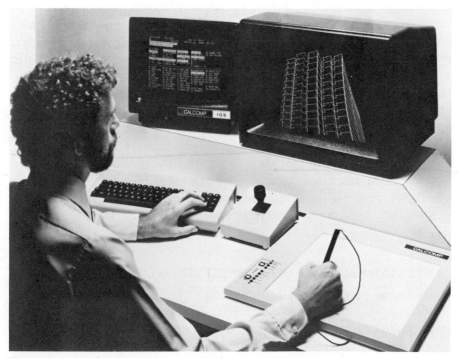

Figure 4. A CalComp minicomputer-based interactive graphics system. (Photograph courtesy of California Computer Products, Inc. (CalComp), Anaheim, CA.)

tubes will become obsolete in CAD/CAM and color raster scan units will predominate.

CIG CAD/CAM units are likely to first prove cost effective in the automotive and aircraft industries. Raster scan CIG will allow the design engineer to specify and then immediately visualize surfaces. CIG devices would be useful for the design of assemblies with interacting parts and in the cross-sectional analysis of parts. Possible applications of this technology are vibration analysis, interference checking, and tool path development.

ARCADE VIDEO GAMES

Some recent arcade video games, such as Gottlieb's REACTOR™ and Sega's ZAXXON™ represent significant advances in graphical presentation, but most games remain pictorially unsophisticated and intellectually unchallenging. Almost any type of CIG training device could be adapted for use in an arcade if its cost could be sufficiently reduced. However, most of the movement now seems in the opposite direction—with arcade games being modified for use as training devices. The Army's Training and Doctrine Command (TRADOC) has completed an extensive study of arcade game technology and its application to military instruction [LUDV81]. Under contract to TRADOC's training support center, Atari has modified their popular "Battle Zone" game into "Army Battle Zone" in which the controls and weapons of the M2 infantry fighting vehicle are replicated. Army experts who have worked with the game find it to be a useful tactical trainer; a more sophisticated version is in the works.

Sanders Associates Inc. (which licenses the basic technology of many of the popular video games) recently shipped a training device to the Army for the M728 combat vehicle. The Army also plans to furnish rooms and off-duty gathering spots for soldiers to play video games based upon the M60 and M1 tanks [LUDV81].

ADDITIONAL MILITARY USES OF CIG TECHNOLOGY

Sensor Image Prediction and Simulation

Image prediction involves the synthesis of a sequence of scenes from a stored database. The simulated images may be thought of as "snapshots" representing scenes at specific locations along the route of a military mission. Such images, when rapidly produced by CIG technology, could be used for premission briefing, in-flight navigation updating, and in-flight target recognition.

Computer-produced imagery could provide a missile navigation system with an expected view, or template, of its flight corridor and target area. The synthetic imagery would be a reference against which a real-time sensor view could be compared for course correction or retargeting purposes.

Synthetic imagery could be supplied to a pilot flying an actual night-time or inclement-weather mission. In-flight mission management information and synthetic terrain scenes would be provided through a head-up, head-down, or helmet mounted display.

Mission Planning and Briefing—Threats and Targets

In a complex battlefield environment, rapid tactical decisions must be made by military commanders on the basis of multiple sets of rapidly changing data. This presents extreme difficulty when the data must be presented and absorbed using conventional maps, charts, photographs, and other graphical aids such as plotting boards. Such media are inflexible, difficult to update, and not easily interpretable if cluttered with data not relevant to the decision-making process.

A hostile environment may include as many as 30,000 potential targets including such major items as tanks, armored personnel carriers, artillery tubes, air defense systems, command posts, and logistic centers. Of the total, about 1000 of these may be high priority targets. It is immediately apparent that there is a significant disparity between the large number of tactical elements present and the major items of concern to the commander. Traditional methods involving the use of hand-delivered paper reports and paper maps with Plexiglas overlays for grease pencil annotation are not well-suited for a rapid flow and culling of information. New techniques are needed to enable commanders to absorb and analyze the mass of information they receive so that they can make decisions which are both timely and correct.

This entire process could be handled by a CIG-type system. The capability must exist for rapidly adding, relocating, and deleting targets and threats from a displayed scene. For this particular task, the locations of these 3-D objects are very important, but the detail to which they are displayed is not. Targets and threats can be displayed symbolically, perhaps color coded. Objects of each type (e.g., tanks or antiaircraft artillery) should be stored in separate files so that they will be available for viewing individually or in combination.

Nap-of-the-Earth Mission Planning

A nap-of-the-earth mission is one in which the flight profile is very near to the ground. Here, the pilot and navigator must be able to rapidly recognize terrain features for mission success and survival. In helicopter nap-of-the-earth missions, the flight path is chosen to take advantage of cover and concealment. Roads, navigable rivers, and other common landmarks are avoided, and routes follow terrain which is inaccessible to other vehicles. To achieve mission success, pilots and navigators must learn to recognize subtle terrain features. Two hours of planning and briefing are often required for a 1-hour mission. These briefings typically employ such aids as maps, charts, photographs, and hand-drawn perspective sketches. A CIG system could be used to supplement or possibly replace traditional briefing material. For this type of mission it is important that the terrain and prominent objects be portrayed accurately. A highly detailed data base for all possible mission areas must be created in advance and stored. It then can be accessed when required to display dynamic imagery viewable from any sequence of locations.

Multisensor Correlation

For some types of military operations, it is important to know how the same scene would appear on different sensor systems. It is paramount that, if computer generated imagery is used for this purpose, it portray the same types of correlations that would appear under actual conditions. Correlation of radar targets and their visually displayed counterparts can be accomplished through the use of separate but similar data bases. Infrared and low-light-level television scenes may also be generated from nearly identical data bases if certain precautions are taken. The need for using slightly different data bases for the different categories of imagery will be explained with several examples. A visual data-base modeler may construct a truck from a set of planar faces, all having the same color. An infrared data-base modeler may note the difference in temperature between the engine compartment and the rest of the truck and treat each part separately. For similar reasons, the regions of an oil tank above and below the oil line must be treated differently in an infrared data base. For a radar data base, objects that are not strong radar reflectors need not even be included.

BRUCE J. SCHACHTER

Columbia, Maryland
February 1983

ACKNOWLEDGMENTS

This book would not have been possible without the help of many individuals and organizations. First and foremost, I extend thanks to my fellow authors of the text.

Material support was supplied by Robert Schumacker of Evans and Sutherland, Johnson Yan of Singer/Link, Kenneth Doris of Gould, Sam Ranjbaran of Advanced Technology Systems, Geoffrey Y. Gardner of Grumman Aerospace, Geoffrey M. Sauter of Aviation Simulation Technology, and several of my friends at General Electric Co. The following also gave assistance and provided material for the book. They have my thanks and appreciation: B. John Shinn, Jim Wurtz, Lew DeWitt, Mike Morrison, James R. Smith; *The Defense Management Journal*, The Singer Co.—Link Division and Link-Miles Division, Society of Photo-Optical Instrumentation Engineers, McDonnell Douglas Corp.—McDonnell Douglas Electronics Co., Conrac Corporation, Advanced Technology Systems—A Division of the Austin Co., Gould Inc.—Simulation Systems Division, Thomas Electronics Inc., Digital Effects Inc., Grumman Aerospace Corporation, Aviation Simulation Technology, General Electric Co., Calcomp—A Sanders Graphics Company, Gottlieb™ Amusement Games, D. Gottlieb & Co., A Columbia Pictures Industries Company, Calma, Evans and Sutherland Computer Co., and Walt Disney Productions.

Special thanks goes to Terry Fleishman for proofreading the manuscript.

Finally, I would like to express my gratitude to my editor David Kaplan and all the other people at Wiley who have worked on the book.

In making a list of people to be thanked, one always runs the risk of leaving someone out. My special thanks and apologies to anyone whose name was inadvertently not mentioned.

B.J.S.

CONTENTS

VLSIC APPROACHES TO COMPUTER IMAGE GENERATION

TRAINING

1 INTRODUCTION

BRUCE J. SCHACHTER

Flight simulators (Figure 1.1) are devices in which air crews can be trained without the use of actual aircraft. In their most sophisticated form, they simulate the instrumentation, vehicular motion and sounds, gravitational forces, radar and electrooptical sensor displays, and out-the-window visuals. The visual flight simulator is that part of the device which presents scenes for the pilot to view out the windows of the mock cockpit.

In early systems, a visual environment was created by movies (Figure 1.2) or video produced by photographing model boards with servodriven TV cameras (Figure 1.3). These approaches are limited in scope and cannot produce true perspective scenes from a wide range of viewpoints. Most modern simulators produce *computer-generated imagery* (CGI).

Computer image generation (CIG) devices are also used in simulators for land, space, and ocean vehicles. All such devices work on the same basic principles, although the data bases from which they generate images necessarily must be different. Visual flight simulation is by far the most important application of CIG and thus is the primary focus of this book.

One way to conceptualize CIG is to imagine a window somewhere in space. The observer looks through this window into a three-dimensional (3-D) world. Now suppose that a line is drawn from the observer's eye through the window, into the 3-D scene. The color of the scene point first intersected by the line is the color "painted" on the window at the point that the line passes through it. Chapter 2 expands upon this intuitive concept and further discusses the fundamental principles of CIG.

Figure 1.1.   Exterior of a flight simulator built by CAE Company.

Chapter 3 investigates design considerations for CIG. This involves determining what are the important features of a scene and how these features can be conveyed to an observer. Since the human visual system is the ultimate recipient of this imagery, it is its needs that must be met, and its limitations that must be understood. CIG devices are designed to provide an effective visual environment for training purposes. The design goal is not image realism. The generated imagery, however, must be of sufficient content, resolution, fidelity, field of view, and brightness for the students to improve their skills.

The established companies in the CIG field are General Electric, Singer/ Link, Evans and Sutherland, and McDonnell Douglas. Each takes a somewhat different approach to system design. However, there are some important similarities worth noting. A geometric data base is always created

Figure 1.2. (a) Exterior of old lunar module procedure simulator (Mission Space Center, Houston, circa 1968). (b) Inside of old lunar lander imaging device. A flying spot scanner scans a 9-inch-wide film strip with a combination of electronic and optical zoom. (Photographs courtesy of Jim Wurtz.)

Figure 1.3. A model board/TV camera system. (Photograph courtesy of Perkin-Elmer Company.)

off-line and stored on magnetic disk. The CIG hardware always is arranged into a pipeline, typically composed of a general-purpose computer, a geometric processor, and a video generator. Chapter 4 reviews the design approaches taken by the major companies, as well as those of several others trying to enter the market.

Digitally generated images have a number of anomalies that are referred to as rastering, aliasing, stairstepping, or "the jaggies." These effects are due to sampling in both space and time domains. Chapter 5 investigates the effects of aliasing on the observer of dynamic scenes. Techniques for eliminating—or at least suppressing—these undesirable attributes are examined.

A data base for a simulator is a model of some region of the world. A model portrays not only the topological and geometric structure of objects and surfaces, but also their color and texture. When a simulated vehicle travels outside the modeled area, the CIG has nothing to show, except possibly some default pattern. Chapter 6 describes approaches to database design.

As the capabilities of simulators increase, customers are demanding the generation of more and more special effects. A CIG is not a video game. Special effects are not for the purpose of entertaining the air crew, but rather they are to add to the simulated conditions under which training can take place. For example, flying in and out of storm clouds is an important part of any pilot's training. An ability to display clouds and lightning allows a simulator to be used in certain training scenarios which would otherwise require an actual aircraft. Military pilots are trained under a much more demanding and diverse set of conditions than civilian pilots—thus military simulators must be able to generate more special effects. Chapter 7 describes some of the required effects and techniques for achieving them.

The continuing evolution of microelectronic devices provides the tools for reducing cost and increasing performance in CIG. In the short term this will be achieved by replacing existing components by new standard components such as microprocessors or VLSI memory chips, or semicustom integrated circuits. For the long term, parallel processing architectures hold the promise of reliability, flexibility, and low cost. However, architectures now being proposed by the university community are generally deficient in some aspect, such as antialiasing, or are not practical because of too long word lengths. Chapters 8 and 9 investigate both near- and long-term solutions to CIG.

Visual simulators bridge the gap between classroom instruction and real-world operations. Their use has increased markedly in recent years. The most obvious reasons are the rising costs of fuel and equipment, safety, and environmental constraints. Chapters 10 to 14 review the role of simulators in training. The essential considerations are cost and effectiveness.

PART ONE

TECHNIQUES AND SYSTEMS

2 COMPUTER-GENERATED GRAPHICS

A Review of Some of the Better-Known Techniques Applicable to Simulation

WILLIAM S. BENNETT

2.1. INTRODUCTION

One way to organize a presentation of the concepts of computer graphics is in the order of increasing complexity of the geometric forms to be shown: points, straight-line segments, "stick-figure" polygons, stick-figure polyhedra, and groups of such polyhedra; then filled polygons, solid-face polyhedra, and finally groups of solid-face polyhedra (Figure 2.1). More complex geometric forms, such as curved-surface patches, are sometimes generated in computer graphics, but a discussion of the above forms will suffice to introduce a number of important problems and their solutions. The interested reader can find a more complete discussion in the book by Newman and Sproull [NEWM79].

This chapter is adapted from an article first published in *SPIE* **59**: *Simulators and Simulation*. (Used by permission of the author and *SPIE*.)

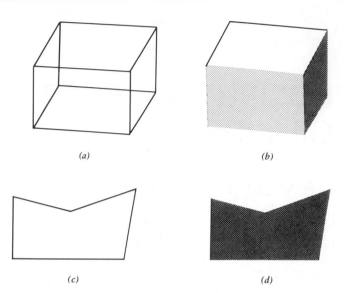

(a)   (b)

(c)   (d)

Figure 2.1. (a) Stick-figure (or wire frame) polyhedron. (b) Solid polyhedron (c) Stick-figure polygon. (d) Filled polygon.

2.2. POINTS

By now the usual way to think of CIG is one that began about 1000 years ago with the Moorish scientist Alhazen. It is to imagine a window placed out in space in front of an observer's eye. What the observer sees through this window is what will eventually be displayed on a screen. Suppose that a straight line is drawn from the observer's eye to a visible surface point in a 3-D world (or data base). Where this line passes through the view window is where the color of the point is to be "painted," that is, it is the perspective projection of the point onto the window (Figure 2.2).

Computing the position of such points on the view window is not difficult if the measurements of Figure 2.3 are available. The two triangles shown are similar triangles, and thus their side lengths are proportional. The computation of the ratio of side lengths contains a division step which cannot be avoided. Figure 2.3 shows a case where only the X dimension is needed. However, in general, both the X and the Y dimensions are needed, so that two divisions are required (Figure 2.4). Things are only this simple if the measurements of the triangles are known. This in turn supposes that the coordinates of all data-base points are known in a coordinate system whose origin is located at the observer's eye, with the Z axis pointing out through the view window, perpendicular to it, and with the X and Y axes parallel to their respective sides of the view win-

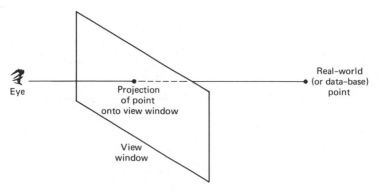

Figure 2.2. Projection of real-world point onto view window.

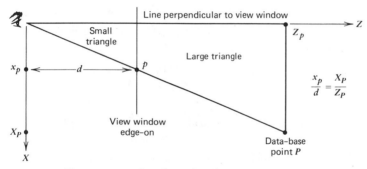

Figure 2.3. Similar triangles in projection.

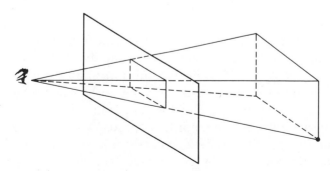

Figure 2.4. Projection triangles for X and Y directions.

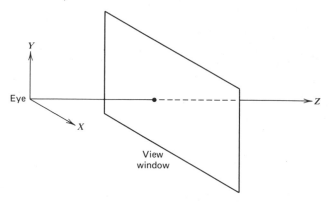

Figure 2.5. Eyepoint coordinate system.

dow (Figure 2.5). If all this is true, then the coordinates of the data-base points are the measurements that are needed.

But consider two facts:

In simulation, the observer must be allowed to move his or her viewpoint and view direction at will.

The data-base modeler would like to be able to encode the data base in some earth-based coordinate system.

These facts imply that the earth-based coordinate system must be transformed to the momentary eye-based coordinate system prior to projection and display. This transformation involves both translational and rotational components, and may also include scaling.

Translation (Figure 2.6) involves moving the center of the earth-based coordinate system to the observer's eyepoint. It requires three additions in 3-D space. Translation can be performed independently of rotation, though combining the two may have some advantages.

Rotation moves the Z axis so that it points away from the eye, and intersects the view window normal to it (Figure 2.7). As a minimum, it requires a matrix multiplication: multiplying the X, Y, and Z values of the data-base point by a 3×3 matrix derived from the angles through which the Z axis is to be moved. This matrix multiplication requires nine scalar multiplications and six additions, and has to be done for every point projected to the view window. Rotation and translation can be combined into one matrix multiplication. For this approach, a 4×4 matrix is used to represent the operation, with the location of a point expressed in homogeneous coordinates, that is, by a 4-element vector containing X, Y, and Z values and a scale factor W (Figure 2.8).

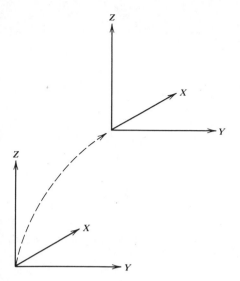

Figure 2.6. Illustration of translation.

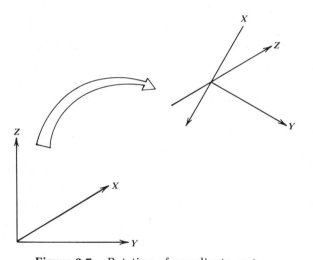

Figure 2.7. Rotation of coordinate system.

$$
(X \quad Y \quad Z \quad W)
\begin{bmatrix}
R_1 & R_2 & R_3 & 0 \\
R_4 & R_5 & R_6 & 0 \\
R_7 & R_8 & R_9 & 0 \\
\hline
T_X & T_Y & T_Z & 1
\end{bmatrix}
= (X_1 \quad Y_1 \quad Z_1 \quad W_1)
$$

Rotation

Translation

Figure 2.8. Matrix multiplication for translation and rotation.

13

	X	Y	Z
1	x_1	y_1	z_1
2	x_2	y_2	z_2
3	x_3	y_3	z_3
4	x_4	y_4	z_4
5	x_5	y_5	z_5
6	x_6	y_6	z_6

Figure 2.9.   A data structure for some points. A six element list.

Thus the computer operations to draw a set of points on the screen involve a matrix multiplication to translate and rotate the earth-axis system to the eyepoint-axis system, followed by the division operations to do the actual perspective projection. The computer needs to have the input data organized into a data structure. For points this can be a list, each entry of which contains an X, a Y, and a Z value (Figure 2.9). Another data structure for a list of points is shown in Figure 2.10. It consists of a series of separate data records, each containing X, Y, and Z values, each pointing to the next record in the list. A pointer to the first entry in the list must reside somewhere in memory. This data structure is not much better than a simple list if the only task is to draw a series of unrelated points. But if more complex figures are to be displayed, it has great utility, as is seen below.

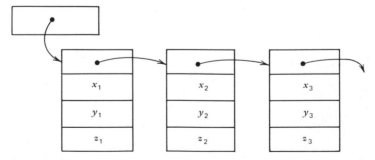

Figure 2.10.   Another data structure for some points. A linked list.

2.3. STRAIGHT LINES

Once it becomes possible to project points to the picture plane, it also becomes possible to project straight-line segments. This is simply done by projecting the line segments' endpoints and then joining them on the picture plane (Figure 2.11). In other words, the perspective projection of a straight-line segment is itself a straight-line segment.

Several methods are available for drawing a line between two points on a cathode-ray tube (CRT). Analog circuitry can be used to move the electron beam continuously along the desired path. Digital generators approximate a line by a series of points on the screen coordinate grid. The electron beam is then deflected in a sequence of discrete steps, of which each step represents a new dot being displayed.

The control of the drawing of straight lines on a screen is done with a computer, often through the use of a display processor. In analog systems, the display processor has commands for turning the beam on and off, positioning it, and controlling its intensity. In digital systems, the display processor has commands for moving the beam incrementally from one grid location to the next.

Projection of a line segment onto the picture plane may result in one end of the segment being off the screen. This can be handled by scissoring (Figure 2.12), in which the CRT attempts to draw the entire line segment, but the beam is blanked out when it tries to draw off the screen. In a second method called clipping (Figure 2.13), a computation takes place to determine where the projected line segment intersects the screen's boundaries, then only that part of the segment actually falling on the screen is presented to it. Scissoring can be inefficient and result in flicker or instabilities. Clipping avoids these problems, but is computationally expensive, although less so in hardware than in software.

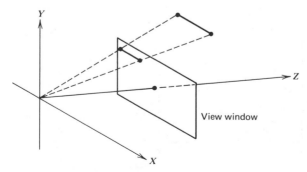

Figure 2.11.   Projection of a line segment onto the view window.

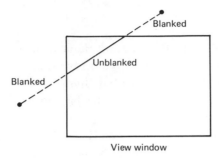

Blanked

Unblanked

Blanked

View window

Figure 2.12. Illustration of scissoring.

An early advance of clipping was the algorithm by Cohen and Suther-land, which operates in two dimensions on the projection plane. It starts by testing a line segment to determine whether it is completely on the screen or completely off. In either case the line segment does not need to be clipped. If the line segment is neither completely on nor off the screen, it is partitioned at one of the screen boundaries and the test is reapplied to each part. The fragment falling outside the screen boundary is deleted. The process is repeated if the remaining fragment crosses another screen boundary.

A later form of the algorithm introduced the concept of dividing the line segment at its center. The rejection or retention of halves proceeds as segments become smaller, finally reaching the precision of the display. This search for the intersection of the line segment with the view window boundaries is logarithmic in computation time. This process is well suited for hardware implementation.

A 3-D form of the algorithm is usually used in simulation. Planes are passed through each of the sides of the view window, each also passing through the viewpoint (Figure 2.14). The planes form a four-sided "pyra-

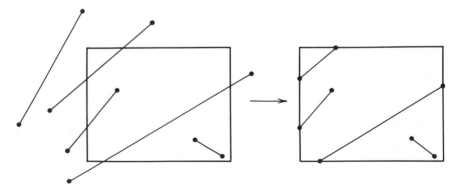

Figure 2.13. Illustration of 2-D clipping.

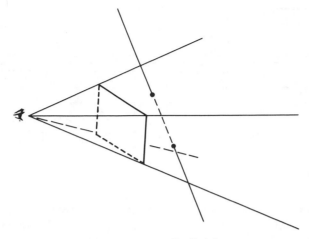

Figure 2.14.   3-D clipping.

mid of vision." Clipping of a line takes place at these planar boundaries, employing the same steps of binary subdivision and trivial rejection as before. When this algorithm is used, projection of line segments to the picture plane follows the clipping process.

Since a straight-line segment is always reconstructed from the projection of its endpoints, a convenient data structure for it is a group of three records: one for the line itself, containing pointers to the ones for the left and right endpoints (Figure 2.15). Programs operating in the display processor utilize this data structure in line drawing commands. The design of good data structures is fully as important as the design of good algorithms in the development of a useful computer-generated graphic system.

The computer operations for the display of a straight-line segment are then (1) the rotation and translation of its endpoints, (2) clipping to establish new endpoints if necessary, (3) projection of the endpoints to the picture plane, and (4) reconnection of the endpoints by a straight line on the picture plane.

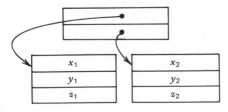

Figure 2.15.   A data structure for a line segment.

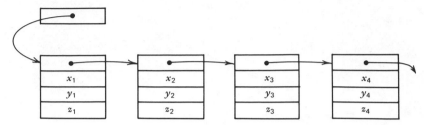

Figure 2.16.   A data structure for a polygon.

2.4.   STICK-FIGURE POLYGONS

A stick-figure polygon can be drawn simply as a series of straight-line segments. A convenient data structure is a chain of records, one for each of the vertices of the polygon, in the order of their traversal (Figure 2.16).

This data structure allows the use of the very elegant clipping algorithm developed by Sutherland and Hodgman [SUTH74b]. It differs from the earlier algorithms in that an entire polygon is clipped first against one bounding plane, and then against another (Figure 2.17) (instead of clipping each polygon edge against all bounding planes and then going on to the next edge). The simplicity that this introduces is striking, especially when a corner of the view window must be used as one of the new vertices of the polygon. This new algorithm accepts the description of a polygon as a series of vertices, and in clipping against a particular bounding plane, proceeds around the polygon asking whether each visited vertex is on the visible or on the invisible side of the plane. If one vertex is visible and the next is not, the intersection of the intervening line segment with the bounding plane is computed, and the resulting new vertex is inserted into the list describing the polygon. Vertices on the invisible side of a bounding plane are omitted, but are used to compute

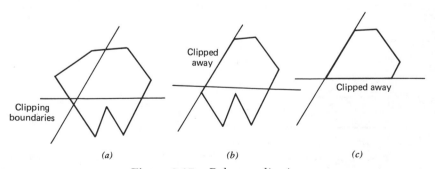

Figure 2.17.   Polygon clipping.

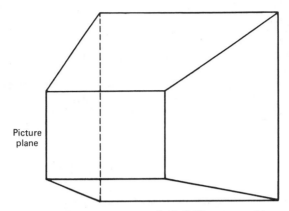

Figure 2.18. Truncated visibility pyramid.

where the polygon reenters the visibility pyramid. The inventors of this algorithm extended it to include two more bounding planes, one coincident with the picture plane and one off in the distance (Figure 2.18).

2.5. STICK-FIGURE POLYHEDRA

A single stick-figure polyhedron can be drawn very simply if hidden lines are not to be eliminated. That is, all its polygonal faces are simply drawn in any order. If back-facing faces are to be eliminated, face normals are computed. The angle between a face normal and the line of sight is inspected. If this angle is obtuse, the face is hidden from the observer's view and can be deleted (Figure 2.19).

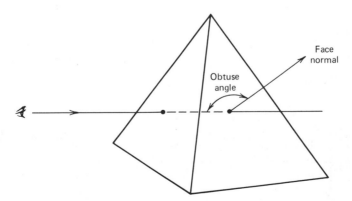

Figure 2.19. Rejection of back-facing faces.

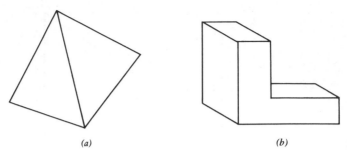

(a)   (b)

Figure 2.20.   Self-occlusion.

This method is sufficient for displaying a single convex polyhedron with its hidden lines removed (Figure 2.20a). For nonconvex polyhedra, front-facing faces may hide other front-facing faces (Figure 2.20b), and the problem becomes more complex.

The data structure for a stick-figure polyhedron can be a single record for the polyhedron itself, pointing to a chain of records, one for each face, with each face record pointing to a chain of vertices (Figure 2.21). Commonly the vertices are arranged in an order which defines the direction of the normal vector so that when it is computed from three of the vertices, it will point away from the polyhedron.

2.6.   GROUPS OF STICK-FIGURE POLYHEDRA

When groups of stick-figure polyhedra are to be drawn, a much more formidable problem immediately arises: determining which portions of

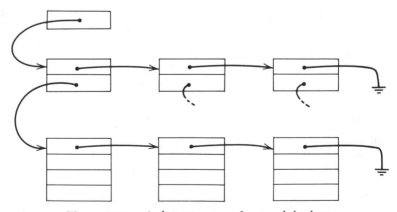

Figure 2.21.   A data structure for a polyhedron.

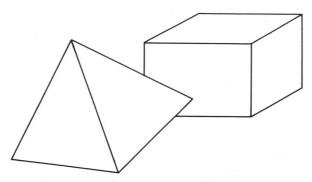

Figure 2.22. Occlusion.

each polyhedron are occluded by other polyhedra (Figure 2.22). Much effort has been expended on this problem in recent years, and several solutions now exist. Since the task is to show the closest object to the eye in each part of the picture, these algorithms have to preserve some kind of depth information. Most do not use slant range to the eye; distance in the Z direction (perpendicular to the view window) is deemed sufficient. One algorithm, which is described below, does not use actual distance directly at all.

One of the most elegant algorithms of this type was developed by Warnock [WARN69]. Warnock introduced the idea of examining the various parts of the viewing screen to determine what, if anything, should be shown. (This is in contrast with those other methods which examine the objects being drawn.) Warnock's algorithm begins by considering the view window as a whole. A test is made to determine if anything is to be shown and also to determine whether a single object occludes all others over the entire window. If so, then that single object is displayed. If not (that is, different objects are closer to the eye in different parts of the screen), the view window is divided into several subwindows (usually four), and the test is repeated on each of these in turn. This process is repeated recursively as far as is necessary (Figure 2.23), more times for those parts of the picture having finer detail. When a subwindow is reached that is of pixel size, the algorithm simply displays a dot at the pixel.

This principle can be applied in conjunction with depth comparisons of varying complexity. The simplest version merely asks whether a subwindow (of whatever size) is completely covered by a face which is closer to the observer than all other faces in that subwindow. If so (for a stick-figure picture), nothing is to be shown. If not, the window must be subdivided again. When the smallest possible window is reached and there is

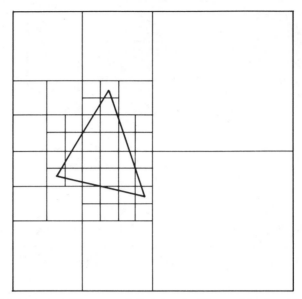

Figure 2.23.   Picture subdivision in Warnock's algorithm.

still not a single face that covers it, then a dot is displayed there. This is sufficient to develop a stick-figure picture with hidden lines removed. This simplest form of the algorithm results in a large number of window subdivisions. More complicated tests are possible, in which features larger than a single pixel are analyzed and drawn directly.

2.7.   FILLED POLYGONS

Filled polygons are projected to the picture plane in the usual manner. However, their straight-line borders are not displayed directly. Instead successive scan lines are swept out to color their interior. These segments can be drawn all at once for a single polygon by zigzagging between its borders (Figure 2.24). Or the colored polygon can be painted out as part of a standard raster scan. In either case it is usual to compute the starting points of scan line segments by applying the slope of their bounding left edge incrementally, so that the starting location of each scan line segment is determined by a simple addition to the location of the one above it. This same method is used to compute the right endpoints of scan line segments. Since a polygon generally has more than one left or right border edge, the edges must be chained together in memory, so that successive edge slopes can be easily retrieved.

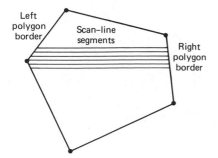

Figure 2.24.   Coloring of a polygon.

In a calligraphic system, all segments for a single face are drawn at once, and this updating of start and stop segment endpoints is all that is needed. However, when the segments are incorporated into a raster scan, all the segments falling on a scan line must be sorted in left-to-right order (Figure 2.25). The sorter which performs this task is a major hardware module in many computer-generated graphic systems.

Data structures for filled polygons can be similar to those used for stick-figure polygons, except that color information needs to be included.

2.8.   SOLID-FACE POLYHEDRA

Occlusion is a major problem when drawing groups of solid-face poly-hedra with a raster scan system. Even after successfully sorting the raster line starts and stops of individual segments of faces, it is still necessary to determine which segments or parts of segments are hidden. Of course, back-facing faces of all polyhedra can be identified with the simple face

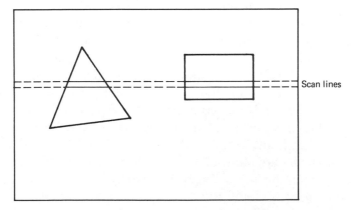

Figure 2.25.   Sorting of scan-line segments in a raster scan system.

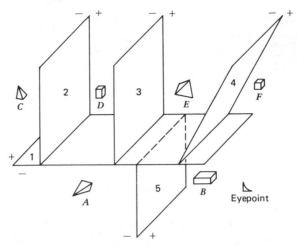

Figure 2.26.   Separating planes. Objects (or clusters) are within pockets bounded by the separating planes. The + and − signs refer to the dot product of the view vector and the surface normals of the separating planes.

normal test, so that if, for instance, the data base is composed of only convex polyhedra, the occlusion problem is only that of determining which polyhedra are in front of which others.

A method devised by Schumacker et al. [SCHU69] allows a large part of the work of hidden-surface elimination to be done off-line and incorporated into the data base. Polyhedra in the data base are separated by a set of invisible "separating planes," which form pockets containing the objects (Figure 2.26). First, a single major plane is passed through the collection of polyhedra, dividing it in two, without cutting through any polyhedron. (It may be necessary to predivide a polyhedron in two to satisfy this last requirement.) Then in each of the resulting halves of the space, a plane is passed dividing the polyhedra there into two groups. This process is repeated until each pocket has only one polyhedron. This structure is stored as a binary tree (Figure 2.27), with the major plane at the top and the polyhedra as leaves at the bottom. The coefficients for the equation of each plane are stored with the record for the plane. In real time the eyepoint is known, and this structure is operated upon to determine on which side of each plane is the eye. A tree-search algorithm yields a list of polyhedra, ordered outward from the observer's eye.

When polyhedra are allowed to be concave, face-against-face methods of occlusion must be used. There are two types, (1) those that use a logarithmic search in depth (the Z direction) and (2) those that use the principle of "clusters" proposed by Schumacker et al. in which the order

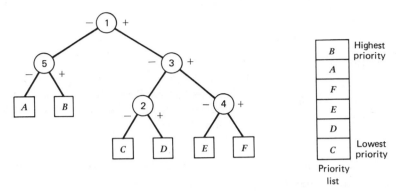

Figure 2.27.   Separating plane tree. Numbers denote separating planes and letters denote objects (or clusters of objects).

of faces within a cluster relative to the eye is unchanged, no matter where the eye is, and only the order of clusters themselves must be determined in real time.

The best known of the former type is Watkin's algorithm [WATK70], which begins by passing planes (one at a time) through both the observer's eye and one of the scan lines of the view window. A plane extends outward (as shown in Figure 2.28) to cut through all data-base faces in its path. The intersection of this plane and a face is a straight-line segment. Projection of such a segment onto a scan line is equivalent to the projection of its encompassing face. Depth information is kept for each segment endpoint that is projected to a scan line. Watkin's algorithm divides a scan line into parts at the boundaries of the segments, and within each of these parts it determines which segment should be shown (based upon

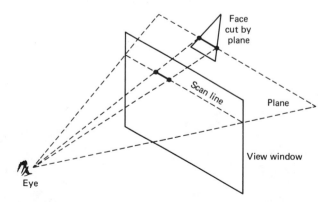

Figure 2.28.   Illustration for scan-line algorithm.

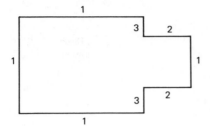

Figure 2.29. Illustration of assignment of priorities. (Higher numbers represent lower priorities.)

depth). This partitioning of a scan line can be done by a binary subdivision which lends itself to hardware implementation.

The second method is Schumacker's cluster algorithm (sometimes called the priority list approach). For this algorithm, during data-base development, entire groups of faces (clusters) are identified for which the occlusion order within a group is totally independent of eye position. A simple 2-D example is shown in Figure 2.29. This priority order is stored in the data base for each cluster, along with planes separating the clusters.

One of the earliest and most comprehensive studies of hidden surface elimination is reported in the paper by Sutherland, Sproull, and Schumacker [SUTH74a]. The reader who is interested in a more complete description of algorithms could do no better than to start there.

3 FACTORS AFFECTING THE DESIGN OF CIG SYSTEMS

BRUCE J. SCHACHTER

3.1. INTRODUCTION

The task of a visual flight simulator is to present the trainee with scenes representative of those that would be seen if the actual mission being trained for were flown. As Bunker [BUNK78] wisely notes, *the goal is not realism, but rather training effectiveness.* The real world is infinitely variable; scenes produced by a CIG device must be only of sufficient content, fidelity, resolution, brightness, and field of view to allow the students to improve their skills. However, if one of these factors falls below the threshold of acceptability, the training value of the device is diminished, if not lost altogether. Not only must the design of a simulator be acceptable for the type of mission being flown, but also it must adequately model the type of aircraft being trained for. A pilot would not want to practice jet fighter missions on a Piper Cub simulator. The design requirements for simulators for high-performance military aircraft far surpass those for civilian aircraft.

In this chapter we review some of the factors affecting the design of visual systems. A number of other factors, which play a prominent role in design, are not covered here. These include cost, design risk, reliability, safety, and availability of hardware components.

3.2. RESOLUTION

The eye's optical system forms an image on the retina. The retina is a field of light-sensitive receptor cells which convert radiant energy into nerve impulses. These impulses travel through the optic nerve to the brain, which transforms them into the sensation of vision. The receptor cells are not uniformly distributed over the retina. Cone cells, which specialize in day and color vision, are most numerous and closely packed in a small depression at the center of the retina, called the fovea. There are three types of cone cells with absorption peaks in the red, green, and blue regions of the optical spectra. Cone cells are intermingled with rod cells, which specialize in twilight vision, toward the retina's periphery.

Visual resolution is the minimum angular separation the eye can see. Visual acuity near and at the center of vision is about 1 arc minute with 20/20 vision, but falls off rapidly toward the retinal periphery. Display resolution is usually measured in minutes of arc per pixel or line. Optical resolution is often measured in arc minutes per line pair.

The resolution of a raster scan display is limited vertically (assuming a horizontal raster) by the number of scan lines (usually 300 to 1024). Horizontal resolution is limited by the 512 to1024 active elements along a scan line. Overall resolution is a function of the distance between pixels, and the size and shape of the light spot at each pixel. A 1000 × 1000 pixel matrix with a 16° × 16° field of view will produce an image with a maximum visual resolution of 1 arc minute. Under ideal conditions this display's resolution will match the eye's resolution. Spreading the pixel matrix out to obtain a wider field of view reduces the resolution of the displayed image.

CRTs used in calligraphic systems usually have a continuous phosphor surface. The electron beam can be moved to address any of 4000 × 4000 or even 8000 × 8000 surface points. Calligraphic displays thus have a much higher resolution than raster scan displays.

Some CIG devices are designed to take advantage of the visual system's ability to capture detail only at the center of vision [LEMA78]. They produce a small, highly detailed area-of-interest scene at the center of vision, surrounded by less detailed imagery. Therefore the line of sight, or at least the direction in which the head is pointed, must be tracked. The area-of-interest approach to scene generation is marked by a number of extremely difficult problems, which must be solved during system design.

3.3.   SHADING

Consider a land form illuminated by both ambient light and direct sunlight. The direction of the sun's illumination can be expressed by its azimuth α and elevation ξ, where azimuth is measured clockwise from

North, and elevation is the angle between the sun's rays and the horizon plane. Let $\mathbf{n}_s$ represent a unit column vector in the direction of the sun, $\mathbf{n}_s$ = (sin α cos ξ, cos α cos ξ, sin ξ)^t.

Some of the light reaching the earth's surface is reflected, while the remainder passes into the ground. The reflected light, as well as the transmitted light, is propagated away from the surface in the form of waves. Both the reflection and the transmission are said to be either diffuse or specular. First, suppose that the surface is a perfect diffuser. A point on a diffusely reflecting surface has the same brightness at every angle of observation. Differences in brightness of patches of the surface are due to differences in the amount of incident light intercepted by the patches, which are at various angles to the light source. According to Lambert's law, the brightness of a diffusely reflecting surface element is related to the product of the intensity of the light source I and the cosine of the incident angle i. A negative cosine value indicates that the light source is on the back side of the face. Surface elements yielding negative terms are not visible if the face is opaque. Let $\mathbf{n}(X, Y)$ denote the unit surface normal at point (X, Y). The diffuse term can be expressed by

$$I_\lambda \max \{0, \mathbf{n}(X, Y) \cdot \mathbf{n}_s\} = \begin{cases} I_\lambda \cos i, & \text{for } |i| < \pi/2 \\ 0, & \text{otherwise} \end{cases}$$

where λ denotes wavelength.

A second component of the reflectance results from treating a surface as a specular reflector. A common model assumes that the majority of light is reflected in a direction making a nearly equal angle of incidence and reflection. For a perfect mirror surface, light only reaches an observer if the surface normal falls halfway between the source direction and the eye direction. For less than perfect reflectors, the amount of specular reflection reaching the eye is related to a power of the cosine of the angle between the direction of reflection and the line of sight. Visual simulators do not portray the specular component of reflection, since modeled surfaces are piecewise planar, making it difficult to display a small surface glare point.

The third component of reflectance is due to ambient light. Ambient light strikes a surface point equally from all directions and thus is reflected equally in all directions.

Simulation of the Lambertian and ambient components of shading will give each nontextured face a uniform color. Gouraud [GOUR71] has shown that the interior of a polyhedral surface can be made to look like that of a curved surface by performing a linear interpolation of shading

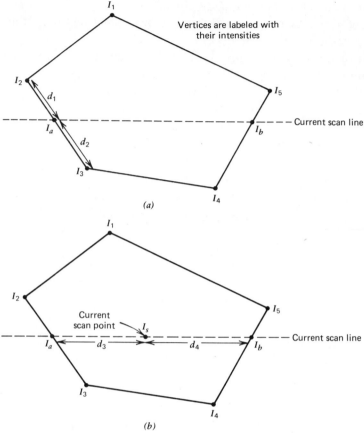

Figure 3.1. Computation steps for Gouraud curved-surface shading. (a) Step 1: compute I_1, I_2, I_3, I_4, and I_5;

Step 2: compute I_a and I_b, where $I_a = I_2 \dfrac{d_2}{d_1 + d_2} + I_3 \dfrac{d_1}{d_1 + d_2}$.

(b) Step 3: compute I_s, where $I_s = I_a \dfrac{d_4}{d_3 + d_4} + I_b \dfrac{d_3}{d_3 + d_4}$.

values (Figure 3.1). This is done by first averaging the surface normals of faces meeting at a vertex. These new normals are used to assign shading values to the vertices. Then as a (convex) face is displayed, the two points at which the scan line intersects its edges are determined, and these points are assigned shading values by linearly interpolating the shading values at their respective edge endpoints. Shading values in the interior of a face are computed by linear interpolations along scan-line segments.

Most visual simulators use curved-surface shading rather sparingly, mainly on the bodies of simulated background aircraft flying through a scene.

3.4. COLOR

Color greatly enhances the intelligibility and perceived quality of an image. Color perception is a powerful mechanism for discriminating among objects which would otherwise appear identical. It is therefore natural to exploit color characteristics as a means of controlling the quality of CGI. Humans can discriminate among at least 100,000 different colors. This suggests the use of at least 7 or 8 bits each of red, green, and blue at each pixel. Mach bands may result in regions where color varies gradually if too little precision is used.

However, if such effects as curved-surface shading and atmospheric attenuation are not considered, one can paint a very good landscape from a palette of a few dozen colors—mostly browns, greens, and blues [HEND49]. Visual simulators take advantage of this by representing the colors of surfaces by codes until the final stages of image generation, where red, green, and blue values are obtained from lookup tables and shading and atmospheric effects are added in.

Since color perception is highest in the foveal region of the retina, it may be acceptable to display scenes with a small, highly detailed color area of interest, surrounded by a less detailed monochromatic backdrop.

3.5. TEXTURE

Natural scenes are rich in texture. The human visual system relies heavily on texture cues to perceive the structure in a scene. Suitable texture control is required to simulate the visual sensations of air speed, height above the ground, tilt of the ground, and location in the environment. Texture provides additional cues for the relative size of objects and their relationships to one another.

The General Electric Company (GE) sells visual simulators which can display textures fitting statistical models [SCHA80a] (see Chapter 7 for details). A number of other companies plan to cover image surfaces with stored sampled aerial photographs.

3.6. SHADOWS

Shadows provide important visual cues. A cast shadow generally indicates that the object casting it is resting on a surface, that the surface is real and actually where it seems to be, and that the object is real and fills a certain volume. Shadows help distinguish up from down, and provide visual cues to the lighting geometry, both of which are crucial to a pilot's understanding of a scene. Shadows cast by one object onto another indicate the objects' geometric relationship in space.

Most systems either do not generate shadows or else they use dark surfaces permanently fixed to the base of polyhedra to represent shadows. Using a very expensive option, some Singer/Link systems can generate shadows as a function of sun position.

3.7. ATMOSPHERIC EFFECTS

The earth's dust and moisture laden atmosphere progressively veils objects, making them grayer and mistier the farther away they are. On a hazy morning, foreground hills are dark and strongly detailed, while the more distant ones fade, one behind the other, until they blend to the sky. The modification to the color C of a surface element due to distance fading is given by the equation

$$C' = C \exp(-\gamma d) + H[1 - \exp(-\gamma d)]$$

where d is the distance to the surface element, γ the fading constant, and H the horizon color.

The location of the horizon and the fading of objects toward it are important visual cues for the sensation of perspective. Visual simulators usually implement a piecewise linear approximation to the fading equation in the last stage of image generation.

Flying among clouds, especially storm clouds, is an important part of any pilot's training (Figure 3.2). Some Singer/Link simulators use opaque polyhedra to represent clouds. Both GE [BUNK77c] and Singer/Link [YAN79] are working on curved object generators which could be used to produce ellipsoidal clouds, possibly translucent [BUNK79b]. This topic is covered further in Chapter 7.

Figure 3.2.   Clouds. (a) Patch of clouds. (b) Cloud surface.

3.8.   DISPLAY OF COMMON OBJECTS

Perception of visual space is built primarily from the spatial relations of objects in the environment. Important visual cues are provided by familiar objects, such as trees, buildings, and vehicles. Depth cues are provided by these objects' relative size, interposition, and change in size when they are approached (what is called the optical flow of visual information). Orientation cues are provided by the vertical alignment of such objects with gravity.

Suppose that the viewing range is only 5 miles (as projected onto the ground) and that the field of view is 45°. If 3 objects per acre are displayed, as many as 18,000 objects could be in view. Even if the scene had nothing else in it but a ground plane, the processing requirements would be far too great for any simulator in use today. Thus the number of objects that can be processed is an important measure of system utility. The available allotment of objects should, of course, be used judiciously. For example, it is prudent to represent a forest by a colored and textured raised surface of tree height, rather than by a million individual trees.

As an aircraft's height above the ground increases, buildings and trees become less important to the pilot as indicators of altitude and distance, while mountains and large areas of vegetation take on a greater significance. As objects appear farther away, it is common to display them in less detail.

3.9. DATA-BASE FIDELITY AND SIZE

A data base for a flight simulator is a model of some region of the world. A data base "drives" the hardware. When a pilot "flies" outside the area modeled by the data base, the simulator has nothing to show, except possibly a default pattern. Commercial aircraft fly between preset locations over a fixed flight path. Military aircraft must be capable of traveling over a large territory at varying altitudes and speeds.

The ground features that a pilot sees in a simulated scene, are modeled to be of the same size, shape, location, and color as their real-world counterparts. This is especially important in and around airports and other special areas of interest. The simulated imagery should be faithful enough to actual conditions to allow the pilot and copilot to "fly" by visual reference.

Data bases for small geographic regions are usually created manually with the aid of interactive computer graphic equipment. An automatic software package is required to economically produce a very large data base. Approaches to data-base design are covered in Chapter 6.

There is currently no standardization of data-base formats among manufacturers, and little between different product lines sold by the same manufacturer; the result is duplication of effort at enormous cost. Although it is not now possible to come up with a single data-base format because of the different topological and geometrical requirements of the algorithms implemented in different hardware, some standardization could be attempted in future systems.

3.10. SCENE CONTENT—DAY SCENES

In all current CIG systems, terrain, culture, and 3-D objects are built from planar faces. Each face has an associated list of attributes, such as color and possibly texture or curved-surface shading. For day scenes, the capacity of a CIG device is generally measured in terms of the number of potentially visible edges that it can process during a frame's time. The processing capacities claimed by manufacturers do not always correspond to the realities of their systems' performance, but more often correspond to whatever their competitors are claiming. The basic problem of how to compare the performance of different systems has not yet been adequately addressed and would be a good research topic.

3.11. SCENE CONTENT—NIGHT SCENES

Night scene content is usually specified in terms of the number of light points that can be displayed. Light points are usually modeled as straight-line strings, with equal spacing between the individual lights of a string (Figure 3.3). A string of lights may, for example, represent those along a road or runway. Some simulators, which are claimed to be capable of displaying $M \times N$ light points, can actually display only M strings with a maximum of N light points per string. If only a single light is to be placed at a location, an entire string will be exhausted. Some devices display lights as squares aligned with the raster. Others do a better job by using circles or Gaussian pulses.

Besides individual light points, a number of other types of lights must also be displayed [AIRM79]. An aeronautical beacon is a visual navigation aid producing flashes of light to indicate the location of an airport, a heliport, a landmark, a significant point of a federal airway in mountainous terrain, or a hazard. Beacons rotate 12 to 60 times per minute in a clockwise direction when viewed from above. Flashes may be of a single color or two alternating colors. Monocolor rotating beacons can be simulated by blinking a single light point at the frequency of rotation. The blinking frequency will be low enough so as not to be affected by the CRT's refresh rate. A beacon alternately flashing two colors can be simulated by two adjacent lights, one of each color. These lights should flash one half-cycle out of phase.

The visual approach slope indicator (VASI) is a system of lights so arranged as to provide visual descent guidance (a glide slope) to the pilot during the approach to the runway. These lights are generally visible from

Figure 3.3. Night scene produced by a GE third-generation visual simulator. (*Note:* This figure appears in color in the color section.)

3 to 5 miles during the day and up to 20 miles at night. VASI lights are highly directional in the vertical direction. The basic principle of the VASI is that of color differentiation between red and white. Each light projects a beam of white light from its upper part and red light from its lower part. Pilots will see the correct combination of red and white only if they are on the proper glide slope. This effect can be achieved by placing hoods constructed from faces around the simulated lights.

Strobe lights at the end of a runway appear to travel at a very high rate. This effect can be simulated by flashing a string of lights on and off in sequence. However, in this case, if the problem is not solved correctly, the intended visual effect will be defeated by the refresh rate of the raster.

3.12.   VIRTUAL OR REAL IMAGE DISPLAY

During an actual flight, the pilot rarely views anything closer than 20 meters. (One exception is aerial refueling [MONR78].) This is true even during takeoffs and landings because of windscreen restrictions. Since the eye's oculomotor adjustments (accommodation and convergence) are used only for seeing objects nearer than 6 meters, anything the pilot views can be regarded as lying at optical infinity [SEMP79].

Visual flight simulators provide the pilot with either a collimated virtual image or a projected real image. A virtual image must be collimated to keep the pilot's eyes directed straight ahead. If a virtual image were not collimated, the pilot would see, for example, a small runway very close instead of a large runway far away. If the collimation is faulty, the pilot will experience motion sickness. Real images are typically projected onto a screen at a great enough distance from the pilot's eyes to make the choice of display type primarily a matter of practicality and economics [SEMP79].

3.13. FIELD OF VIEW [SEMP79]

In general, field of view (FOV) requirements for central vision relate to the pilot's use of the front and adjacent side windows. The view through the front windows is used mainly for navigation, terrain avoidance, and object recognition. The view through the side windows helps in detecting objects and movement, and in judging lateral distance. Peripheral vision through the side windows is the primary source of information for body orientation, direction of travel, and approximate rate of travel. A wide FOV is necessary for tasks demanding an ability to continuously detect altitude and altitude changes, direction of travel, changes in the direction of travel, approximate speed, and objects entering view from the side. A wide FOV is particularly important for roll and bank control.

Military simulators used for combat training generally require a very wide FOV. The pilot must make quick and drastic maneuvers in response to objects approaching from all directions. Ship's bridge and land vehicle simulators may also require a wide FOV.

3.14. BRIGHTNESS AND CONTRAST CONTROL

Contrast sensitivity depends upon the intensity of illumination. At high levels, acuity is greatest near the center of vision but decreases rapidly toward the periphery. The eye is not good at perceiving absolute brightness and contrast levels, but it is extremely good at locating the boundaries between different brightness or contrast regions. For a system with multiple displays, the brightness and contrast characteristics of adjacent displays must be well matched.

3.15. REFRESH AND UPDATE RATES

Two related terms are refresh rate and update rate. Refresh rate refers to the rate at which a set of phosphor dots is addressed; update rate is the rate at which the image is recomputed to reflect a new observer position.

The impulse response of the human visual system increases with increasing luminance. With a very bright (approximately 100 foot-lambert) double-pulse light source, integration is complete when onset-to-onset asynchrony is below 20 milliseconds. This translates to a refresh rate of 50 times per second, a minimum that ensures that even small bright objects moving across a screen will not flicker because of an insufficient refresh rate (though flicker or similar problems may be caused by other effects, some of which are described in Chapter 5). For a system with low brightness (10^{-2} to 10^{-1} foot-lamberts) 20 times per second may be sufficient.

Standard TV is refreshed at a rate of 30 frames per second, formed from 60 fields, with $2:1$ interlacing to reduce flicker. That is, all odd rows of the image are scanned out in one $\frac{1}{60}$-second period, then all even rows in the next $\frac{1}{60}$-second period. TV images are updated continuously as a moving scene is captured by a TV camera. Many visual simulators use the same refresh rate as standard TV, but with a field rate update. This scheme appears to offer a reasonable balance between cost and image quality. The relationship between TV and CIG is discussed further in the Appendix to this chapter.

3.16. OVERLOAD RESPONSE

For optimum efficiency, CIG systems are designed to operate near their maximum capacity. This means that even a properly designed image generator will occasionally become overloaded. When this happens, image quality should degrade gracefully. Approaches to overload management include: removing very small objects, reducing the level of detail to which objects are displayed, generating fewer scan lines (each spread out), decreasing the sampling interval along a scan line, eliminating subpixel sampling, and slowing the update rate.

3.17. HEAD ENVELOPE

Head envelope is the space in which pilots can move their heads without the scene degenerating to a point where performance is affected. Some displays require pilots to keep their heads nearly stationary. Others can produce a good display for pilots and copilots separated by 3 feet.

3.18.   NUMBER OF CHANNELS

Each window of a simulator viewed by a single observer requires an independently calculated moving image. The same geographic region which is viewed through the front window will moments later appear moving past the side windows. A commercial aircraft simulator typically requires three to four channels to present views for the front and adjacent side windows. One common commercial configuration is a 3-channel, 4-window system, where the pilot and copilot get identical forward views (Figure 3.4). To produce the wide field of view typical of military aircraft, 3 to 10 channels are required. A simulator for an electrooptical sensor, radar display, optical tracker, periscope, or spacecraft porthole requires only one channel. An image generator designed to produce animated cartoons would also require only one channel.

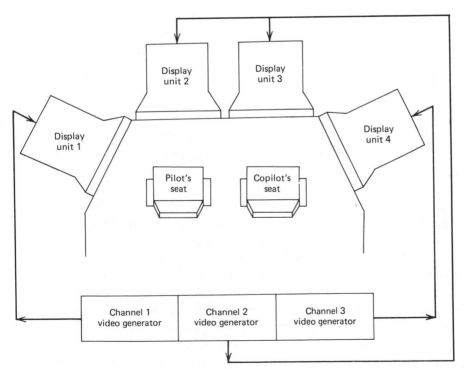

Figure 3.4.   Configuration of a 3-channel, 4-window visual simulator.

3.19. CHANNEL ALIGNMENT

When separate displayed images are juxtaposed to create a wide field of view, care must be taken to prevent discontinuities at the boundaries between images. This is usually less of a problem for multiple virtual images than for geometrically corrected real images displayed on the inside of a dome.

3.20. NUMBER OF COCKPITS

Military simulators sometimes link two cockpits together so that their pilots can practice aerial combat, formation flight, and other joint maneuvers (Figure 3.5). Each of the simulated aircraft appears as a moving model within the displayed scene of the other. These aircraft images respond to the action taken by their "pilots."

APPENDIX: TV AND CIG

A monochromatic television picture tube (called a Cathode-Ray Tube or CRT) consists of a highly evacuated funnel-shaped bottle, inside of which are a screen and an electronic scanning mechanism (Figure 3.6). The viewing screen is located on the inside front face of the bottle. The neck at the back end of the bottle contains an electron gun. At the rear of the gun is a heated cathode which emits a stream of electrons which form into a cloud of free electrons. These electrons are shaped into a beam by an aperture in a control grid surrounding the cathode. The electrons are accelerated by one or more positive grids and are focused to a spot on the screen by an electrostatic or magnetic lens. The strength of the electron beam is modulated by the potential on the control grid, which varies in accordance with the video signal transmitted by the TV station. The focused beam is deflected by a yoke, which can again use either electrostatic or magnetic principles. After deflection, the electron beam travels in a straight line, through a uniform field created by a high positive potential to its target spot on the screen. The screen consists of a continuous layer of phosphor particles. When electrons strike a spot on the screen, a fraction of their kinetic energy is absorbed by molecules of the phosphor surface exciting them to a higher energy state. A photon of visible light is emitted as each excited electron returns to its natural state.

The electron beam draws out a succession of nearly horizontal straight-

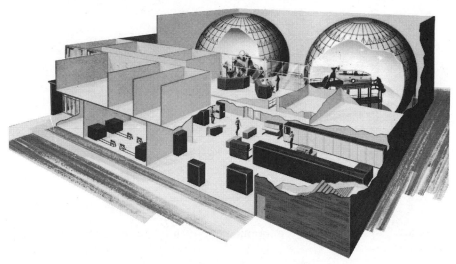

Figure 3.5. Depiction of McDonnell Douglas air combat maneuvering simulator. (Courtesy of Gould Company.)

line segments, each formed left to right (as viewed from in front of the TV), the lines following in sequence from top to bottom. This process is known as the scan out of the image and is similar in motion to a human's visual scan of a printed page. The instantaneous location of the beam on the screen is known as the scan spot, the path it follows as the scanning pattern or raster. In the United States 525 raster lines form a complete picture. Each picture is formed by two top-to-bottom sweeps, each constituting one field. A field thus has 262.5 lines. The scan lines of the first field are laid out so that an equal empty space is maintained between successive lines. The lines of the second field fall within this empty space (Figure 3.7). Two fields constitute one frame; and there are 60 fields scanned out per second, the pairs of which form 30 frames per second.

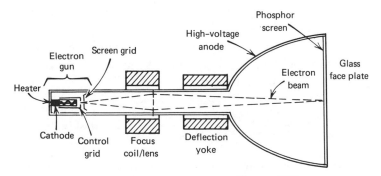

Figure 3.6. Components of basic CRT.

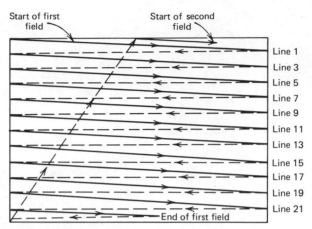

Figure 3.7. Raster scan pattern for one field of an interlaced CRT. Dashed lines denote retrace.

The 60 field per second rate was originally chosen to correspond to the 60 cycle per second (hertz) rate of electric line current, in order to avoid power line "beat" interference on the TV screen. The frequency rate of alternating current was itself chosen to prevent the perception of light bulb flicker.

Upon reaching the end of a horizontal scan line, the electron beam snaps from the right edge to the left edge of the screen. During this retrace, the horizontal sync pulse transmitted by the station turns off the beam. This pulse also synchronizes the start of each line trace in the receiver with that of the transmitter. Similarly, at the end of each field, a vertical sync pulse signals the electron beam to return to the top of the screen and start the next field. Although this pulse is much longer than the horizontal one, it is off the screen and out of sight in a properly working receiver. If a TV's vertical hold is not adjusted correctly, a black bar will roll through the picture—this bar is in fact the vertical sync signal.

Since 525 lines are transmitted in $\frac{1}{30}$ second, there are 64 microseconds available for a line scan. However, up to 15 percent of this may be consumed in the horizontal retrace motion. This leaves only about 54 microseconds for the active reproduction of as many as 435 pixels per line. This represents a maximum rate of

$$\frac{435 \text{ pixels}}{\text{scan line}} \frac{1 \text{ scan line}}{54 \times 10^{-6} \text{ seconds}} = 8 \times 10^6 \text{ pixels per second}$$

Two pixels can be approximated by one cycle of a transmission signal. The receiver must therefore operate at 4 MHz. In the United States a

6-MHz bandwidth is reserved for each TV channel, which is sufficient for video plus audio plus a buffer between stations.

A CIG device produces digital picture data. Thus a digital-to-analog (D/A) converter is needed to put the data into the form required by a CRT. An 8-bit D/A converter can produce a 256-step signal corresponding to 256 monochrome levels. Since CIG is stairstepped, it is not really equivalent to the true analog signal captured by a TV camera. In CIG each digitally generated stairstep or pulse must be targeted to a particular spot on the screen. To maintain this relationship, data must be generated by the CIG, or read out of memory, at the exact rate required to drive the CRT; or conversely the CRT must be built specifically to accept data of a certain format and rate, or a combination of both.

A monochromatic monitor can be built to write strokes across the screen in any direction. With high-speed analog circuitry and deflection yokes, very fast writing speeds can be achieved. This calligraphic approach can be used to draw out a scene, and is especially appropriate for night scenes where the beam is directed to paint out light points. This approach generalizes to color with the use of beam penetration tubes.

Multicolored beam penetration tubes were considered for use in early TVs, but the idea was soon abandoned due to color limitations. They have, however, found application in CIG (mostly for night/dusk systems). These CRTs exploit the penetration of electrons into materials as a function of their kinetic energy.

Two layers of phosphors with different characteristics are deposited on the face plate of a CRT. Depending upon the velocity of energy of the bombarding electrons, this being a function of the accelerating voltage, the electrons can be made to penetrate and be absorbed by either or both phosphor layers. Typical beam penetration tubes place a barrier layer between phosphor layers or around the particles of one to provide a distinct separation between the anode voltages required to excite the layers. The spectral characteristics of the emitted light will depend on the spectral characteristics of the phosphors and the energy absorbed by each. If

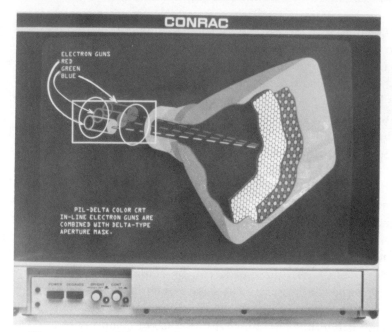

Figure 3.8.   A Conrac precision in-line gun color monitor.

one phosphor layer is red and the other is green, the emitted light will be either red, green, or some yellow to orange hue. Multicolor scenes are painted out by rapidly switching the CRT's anode voltage level as the beam draws out strokes.

Much of the preceding discussion holds for full-color receivers. The major difference is that color TV picture tubes usually have three independent electron guns. These are closely spaced within the neck of the tube and use a common deflection yoke. Each gun has its own heated cathode to emit electrons, its own control grid to modulate the intensity of the beam, and a focus mechanism. Three sets of phosphor dots or bars coat the inner frontface of the tube. One of these emits red light when struck by the electron beam, another emits blue light, and a third emits green. A red, green, blue triad forms one picture element.

The three beams are focused to pass through holes in a shadow (or aperture) mask placed just inside the screen. By controlling the strength of the three electron beams separately, the three primary colors emitted by a triad of phosphor dots are blended to produce the desired visual color.

There are a number of ways that the phosphor dots can be organized. The configuration of the delta–delta system provides the highest color resolution available in raster scan CRTs. The red, green, and blue guns are arranged in a triangle and are aimed at the round holes of the mask. The critical factor in determining resolution is the "pitch" or space between the holes in the shadow mask. Home TV uses a nominal shadow mask pitch of 0.92 mm. Ultra-high-resolution graphic monitors have a pitch of 0.31 mm or less.

In the in-line gun system the three color guns are side by side. The phosphors are laid out in vertical stripes, and the electron beam is directed through slots in the shadow mask. This technology lowers monitor costs by eliminating the expensive dynamic convergence controls needed in delta–delta systems.

The precision in-line system uses a hybrid approach (Figure 3.8). An in-line gun configuration is used, but with the type of fine pitch shadow mask and tri-dot phosphor structure used in delta–delta CRTs. Like the in-line CRT, precision in-line monitors do not require dynamic convergence controls.

Color CRTs used in CIG are specially designed at a cost of two orders of magnitude greater than those built for the home. They must meet very rigid standards of uniformity and quality.

For a further discussion of these topics see [CONR80] and the *Encyclopedia Britannica* entry on television.

4 COMPUTER IMAGE GENERATION SYSTEMS

BRUCE J. SCHACHTER

4.1. OVERVIEW

Let us informally consider how to design a CIG system for flight simulation. The data base obviously has to be 3-D so that a pilot can fly through it and view it from any direction. What should a data base contain? First of all, the pilot has to take off from a runway and fly over terrain. The land surface should consist of mountains, rolling hills, and flat areas. The color of the ground should mainly be determined by the lakes, rivers, and vegetation located on it. Buildings, trees, and other 3-D objects also must be modeled.

One convenient way to construct the ground surface is from flat pieces, almost like pieces of cardboard cut up and glued together. Triangles are a good choice for the shapes of these pieces, because they fit together well in 3-D space whereas, for example, rectangles do not.

One way to color the ground would be to "paint" each triangle a different color. However, the locations and shapes of surface features are not likely to coincide with the triangular components of terrain. Colored polygons resting on the triangular surface will do a better job of representing culture. Since adjacent triangles are not likely to be coplanar, polygons must first be broken up into fragments before being put onto the terrain. No fragment can cross an edge of a triangle.

The 3-D objects also have to be portrayed. An object can be conveniently modeled by a polyhedron, or by several attached polyhedra separated by planes. A polyhedron consists of a number of planar facets (or faces for short), with the topological relations between adjacent faces specified.

The data base once constructed has to be stored on a medium for easy access by the CIG. Magnetic tape is not suitable for quick retrieval. Core is too expensive and not portable. Magnetic disk can hold a fairly large data base and allows quick access. Optical disk is also now available. It has a very large storage capacity, but is not erasable. An optical disk and a magnetic disk can be placed in tandem, with the optical disk holding the bulk of the data base and the magnetic disk holding updates, corrections, and the directory. The data base must be partitioned into moderately sized units when stored on disk. This will allow the CIG to retrieve only that part of the data base which is needed at any point in time, as determined by the pilot's location and view direction.

A CIG is actually a special-purpose computer hooked up to a host flight simulator. Like many computer devices, it has a controller. The controller's tasks include monitoring the simulated aircraft's position and attitude, communicating with the instructor's station, and managing the image generation hardware. As the pilot approaches a new geographic region, the controller reads the data from the disk to describe the region.

The function of the rest of the CIG is to convert the input data into visible scenes for the pilot (and possibly copilot) to see out the windows of a mock cockpit. A typical aircraft has two front windows and four side windows. A pilot and copilot can be presented identical scenes to view out the forward windows. Each side window requires a different scene.

A CIG device which displays five 1000×1000 pixel color images simultaneously at TV rates has to generate about 10^9 bits per second. This requires 10^9 to 10^{10} computer operations per second. This is more computational power than is available with a general-purpose computer. Computer architects resort to two well-known techniques to achieve the required performance [KOGG81], pipelining and parallelism.

All current CIG devices use a pipelined architecture. Pipelining involves splitting the operation into separate pieces and allocating individual hardware units to each piece (Figure 4.1a). As an item of data flows through the pipeline, it occupies one stage at a time. The inputs to each stage come almost entirely from the output of the previous stage. Basically, other than the exchange of inputs and outputs, there is no data transfer between stages. Data travel from one stage to the next according to the "tick" of a clock. The rate at which video images leave the pipeline depends strictly on the maximum time required to traverse any single stage and not on the number of stages. The time required for a data item to traverse all stages is called the throughput delay of the pipeline.

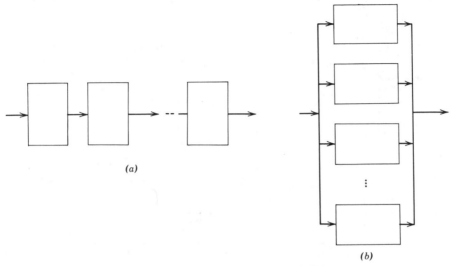

Figure 4.1. (a) Pipelining. (b) Parallelism.

Parallelism emphasizes concurrency by replicating a hardware unit a number of times (Figure 4.1b). High performance is obtained by having all units operating simultaneously. In its purest implementation, a device is composed of identical units, operating in parallel, each performing identical functions on different parts of the data. A less pure implementation consists of the same or different units operating in parallel, each performing different operations.

The goal of designing a computer system using pipelining or parallelism is clearly performance. If some task can be executed with straightforward design in C seconds, it may be possible to break it up into N subtasks, running on a parallel or pipelined system, and obtain an output every C/N seconds. Although pipelining and parallelism may appear to originate from opposite philosophies, in real CIG systems the contrast is not very sharp, and often an architecture combines both technologies. A CIG system typically consists of three pipelined stages (Figure 4.2). The first stage is the controller which usually takes the form of a general-purpose 32-bit computer (e.g., VAX, SEL, Perkin-Elmer). The second stage is typically a special-purpose computer entailing some degree of parallelism. Its duties include such geometric processing tasks as perspective projection, hidden-surface elimination, clipping, and video channel assignment. The third stage is the video processor which converts a 2-D digital scene description into analog video.

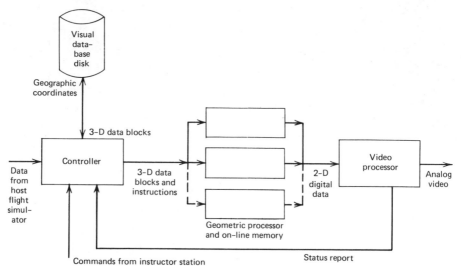

Figure 4.2. Block diagram of a typical computer image generator.

4.2. CIG SYSTEMS

As of 1982, CIG devices built by only four companies are in use in training programs: General Electric, Singer/Link, Evans and Sutherland, and McDonnell Douglas. Several other companies are trying to enter the market. We will review the design and operation of the major systems produced and in development.

The descriptions given here are as the various companies present them in the referenced documents. It should be realized that most devices exist in a variety of forms; a basic product is often tailored to meet the requirements of a particular training program. Furthermore, after a simulator is installed, follow-on activities often improve its performance and add to its capabilities. For example, the GE AWAVS system started out as monochrome with a 1000-edge capacity [MARR77, COLL78]. Recently it has been converted to full color, its edge capacity has been doubled, corrections have been added to compensate for distortions caused by its dome display [CORO80], and its name has been changed to VTRS.

In many companies' advertising literature, photographs taken from working systems are freely intermingled with photographs taken from laboratory setups, composite photographs, or even scenes created by an artist with an airbrush. A number of these photographs have found their way into the computer and popular literature. An attempt is made here to present only photographs taken from actual working systems.

4.2.1. General Electric Company

The first CIG device was built by GE's Electronics Laboratory in the late 1950s. It used a calligraphic display and analog circuitry to produce a repeated pattern over a ground plane. Its main significance was to prove the feasibility of real-time graphics.

In 1962 GE was funded by NASA to design and build a CIG device suitable for training. The concept was developed to place polygonal ground features and polyhedral objects onto a flat earth. Early versions of this device displayed little more than a checkered earth surface. The capability for displaying simple objects began in the mid 1960s and progressed toward the late 1960s. Although true perspective scenes were generated, many visual artifacts were present to distract the viewer. No edge smoothing of any kind was employed. Although separate scenes observable from a single viewpoint were displayed, no attempt was made to combine them into a single scene with a wider field of view. The operation of these GE second-generation machines is covered in more detail in Section 4.2.1.1.

GE's third-generation technology was first used in a visual flight simulator called advanced development model (ADM) or 2F90. It was delivered to the Navy in 1972. It was intended for use as an instrument to measure the effectiveness of CGI in pilot training. Three channels were combined to provide the pilot with a 60° vertical by 180° horizontal field of view. Three GE light valves projected the separate images toward the viewpoint. The system displayed a rather sparse 500-edge scene. The setup of the mock cockpit, display screens, and light valves is depicted in Figure 4.3.

A 1973 report by O'Conner, Shinn, and Bunker [OCON73] describes the successes and failures of ADM. The 500-edge limitation and lack of texturing was found to provide inadequate velocity and attitude cues for lineups and landings on both airfields and aircraft carriers. On the positive side, the simulation of haze provided important visual cues and enhanced scene quality. In the original data base the aircraft carrier deck was dark and the landing area markings were a high-contrast white. When viewed from a distance, quantization effects caused the white stripes to scintillate and move about abruptly as they intercepted different scan lines and pixels. This problem was overcome by coloring the entire landing area white and overlaying low-contrast gray deck markings. Perspective cues were enhanced by placing a broad checkerboard pattern over the ocean surface surrounding the aircraft carrier. This is a good example of a case where decreasing realism increased training effectiveness.

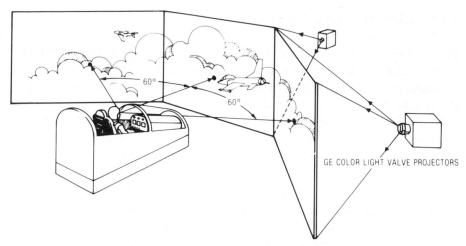

Figure 4.3. GE ADM display approach.

Naval device 2B35 is similar to ADM. The same display concept is used with the horizontal field of view increased to 210°. The device generates 1000 edges and 1000 light points. The data base for this simulator concentrates scene detail to the vicinity of the runway and target areas. Moving clouds are displayed, with the pilot's visibility reduced upon entering a cloud.

An advanced simulator for undergraduate pilot training (ASUPT) was delivered to the Air Force in 1974. The device displays 2500 edges at once; these edges are smoothed in the horizontal direction only. Each ASUPT mock cockpit is built within a geodesic support structure (Figure 4.4). Seven of the twelve faces of the supporting dodecahedron have 36-inch monochrome CRTs in line with Pancake Windows™. This configuration produces a ±150° horizontal by +110°, −40° vertical field of view. This was the first CIG device to use wraparound infinity optics with no breaks between channels.

ASUPT was designed as an advanced research device for exploring the role of simulators in pilot training. The ASUPT system was the most sophisticated in the world at the time of its introduction. It has been studied extensively to obtain insights which could be applied to the design of future devices. On the positive side, ASUPT's wide field of view allows a student pilot to undertake missions which cannot be attempted on devices with a narrower view field. However, ASUPT's high-contrast monochromatic display has received some criticism. The observable resolution of 7 arc minutes is sufficient for most tasks not requiring precision flying. However, only in areas where scene content is concentrated is it possible to undertake low-altitude flight, or tasks requiring precise depth perception. Furthermore, objects of similar intensity and shape are sometimes confused in identification. It is thought that if the imagery could be displayed in full color, the resolution, although still marginal, would no longer be a limiting factor.

ASUPT displays 3-D objects with exceptional clarity. They have been shown to be excellent references for ascertaining correct altitude, rate of altitude change, location in the environment, and alignment with the runway. However, as is typical of simulators of this era, the pilot is occasionally distracted by objects popping in and out of view. For example, as

(a)

Figure 4.4. (a) ASUPT system. *(Figure is continued on page 54.)*

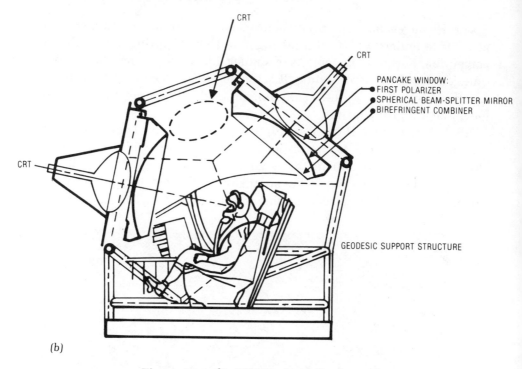

(b)

Figure 4.4.   *(b)* ASUPT visual display unit.

the runway is neared, hangars, trees, and runway surface markings may pop into view, as the edges required to construct them become available as other objects pass out of view. ASUPT is covered in more detail in Section 4.2.1.2.

The first day/night full-color visual flight simulator for commercial aircraft was delivered to Boeing in 1975 for their 700 series of planes. This unit can display 1000 edges and 2000 light points at a 30 frame per second update rate. It has three display channels, each having a 40° horizontal by 30° vertical field of view. The narrow vertical field of view has proved adequate for straight-in approaches to runways, but not quite satisfactory for some other maneuvers. The resolution and clarity of the displayed image are good, and depth perception is excellent. The major special effects simulated are cloud cover of variable thickness, patchy scud clouds, and atmospheric attenuation. An upgraded version delivered in 1978 for the 747 aircraft displays 4000 edges and 2000 light points (Figure 4.5).

GE delivered an aviation wide-angle visual system (AWAVS) to the Navy Training Center in Orlando, Florida, in 1978. The simulator trains pilots for aircraft carrier takeoffs and landings. Its CIG produces 1000

Figure 4.5. (a,b) Scenes produced by the GE Boeing visual simulators. (a) also shows the inside of the 747 simulator cockpit. (*Figure is continued*.)

Figure 4.5.   (c) The Boeing 747 simulator cockpit viewed from the outside.

edges and 2000 light points. The display is a monochrome wide-angle real image appearing on the inside of a 10-foot-radius dome. The entire display system, consisting of the screen, two TV projectors, and a Fresnel optical landing system projector (FOLSP), is mounted on a mock cockpit on top of a motion platform (Figure 4.6). The FOLSP projects the target image (aircraft carrier), which can be superimposed on a background seascape or inset into it. The 160° background seascape can be centered at the aircraft or offset 40° to the left. This approach has many difficulties associated with it. Very complicated transforms are required to compensate for the distortion resulting from the dome display. When the system is used in the inset mode, part of the background seascape must be blanked out so that the foreground image can be inserted into it. It is very difficult to obtain a smooth transition between the separate images.

In 1977 GE began putting together an automated data-base development system [CUNN80]. While most early GE visual units were intended for training in and around airports and other locales of special interest, fourth-generation devices were to display large geographic areas to sufficient detail to support low-altitude flight. Cunningham and Picasso expect this trend to continue. They state that "the ultimate goal (at GE) appears to be the manufacture of aircraft simulators capable of global flight paths arbitrarily selected by the flight instructor." They show (Figure 4.7) that the number of displayed edges plus light points has been growing at a near exponential rate for GE devices. The sizes of GE data bases have not followed suit—this is because through the 1960s and 1970s they have been hand-modeled.

GE's automated data-base development system was completed in 1979 [CUNN80, SCHA80a]. The inputs to the system are U.S. Defense Mapping Agency Digital Land Mass terrain and culture files. A terrain file is an

Figure 4.6. (a) AWAVS outside of spherical dome and motion platform. (AWAVS has recently been renamed VTRS.) (b) View from inside. (*continued* .)

57

Figure 4.6. (c) VTRS model for OR1 auxiliary oiler. (Ship modeled by M. Morrison, N. Snyder, and F. Sica of GE.)

array of elevation values for a given geographic area. The associated culture file holds encoded descriptions of the man-made and ecological surface features residing within the terrain region. Most feature types are represented by a polygonal boundary and descriptor table. The table includes such information as land use (e.g., forest), predominant makeup (e.g., coniferous trees), and average height. The locations of some man-made features such as bridges, dams, walls, and pipelines are specified by polygonal lines, while others such as water towers and tall buildings have their location and height specified. GE's data-base development software first partitions the raw data into manageable blocks. Then a digital Wiener filter is used to locate points of significance (peaks, pits, saddle points, and ridge line segments) on the terrain surface. Next a hierarchy of triangular faceted surfaces is fitted to each block of raw terrain data. Each of these piecewise planar approximations corresponds to a different level of detail to which the terrain is modeled. The culture polygons are also approximated to different levels of detail by standard computational geometric techniques. Each level of detail of culture data is then placed on

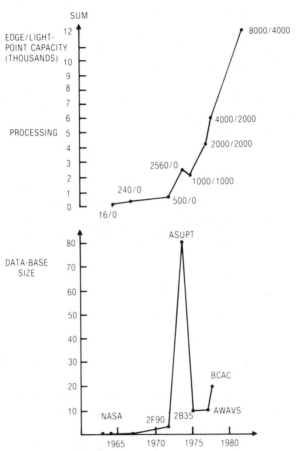

Figure 4.7. Processing capacity versus data-base size at GE. (From [CUNN80].)

top of (i.e., intersected with) the corresponding terrain level of detail. The locations of generic objects are also placed into the data base.

This automatically generated data base covers most of the geographic area modeled. However, data describing airports and other areas of special interest are created or augmented manually with standard interactive computer graphic techniques. Certain special models, such as important buildings and bridges, are also created by hand and are placed into their correct locations in the environment model. Moving models, such as planes and rockets, are also prepared by hand. The manually and automatically generated components of the data base are eventually merged and placed onto the visual data-base storage disk. The total geographic region covered is called the gaming area (at least for military systems).

The first GE fourth-generation device was their B-52 visual simulator (Figure 4.8). It was delivered in 1980 with a 250,000-square-mile data base automatically constructed from Defense Mapping Agency data and five hand-modeled day, dusk, and night airfield data bases. The next fourth-generation system was built in 1981 for a C-130 aircraft simulator. It is covered in detail in Section 4.2.1.3.

4.2.1.1. GE Second-Generation Systems

GE was funded by NASA in 1962 to develop a flight simulator for the Apollo program. A system was delivered in 1963 which displays a simple texture over a ground plane (Figure 4.9). An improved version built in the mid 1960s is called the visual three-view space flight simulator [GE] (Figure 4.10). It displays three perspective views on three circular RCA color shadow-mask CRTs. The three views appear in three nonabutting space-craft portholes, two with a 60° circular field of view and the third with a 25° circular field of view.

For the perspective calculations, the vehicle is assumed to have no roll with respect to the raster. The geometric calculations involve projecting the current scan line onto the ground plane or, to get an equivalent result, projecting the endpoints of the scan line. The line segment joining these endpoints is partitioned into 256 smaller segments of equal length.

Binary square mosaic textures are stored by plug-in hardwired diode matrix boards called map tables. The video is generated by scanning the map tables in synchrony with the raster scan. For each video pulse period (approximately 0.2 microsecond) the position in a map table is advanced an amount corresponding to the length of one small segment. The color value computed for the current map index is then assigned to the scan pixel.

Each texture T is stored at four component levels of hierarchy, denoted by T_1, T_2, T_3, and T_4, where T_1 is the finest texture component. The four are combined by modulo 2 addition when generating the pattern appearing on the ground plane near the viewpoint. Each successively coarser component is faded out in a zone determined by slant range from the viewpoint. The finest component is faded in zone 1, followed by the next finest in zone 2, and so on, until, toward the horizon, only the coarsest component remains. The coarsest component fades toward a background color at the horizon. No attempt is made to smooth the edges of the colored texture squares.

Figure 4.8.   Several scenes produced by the GE B-52 visual simulator. Note the excellent texture on surfaces. (Part *a* of this figure is reproduced in color in the color section.)

(a)

(b)

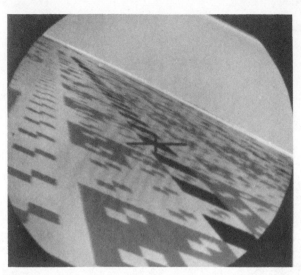

Figure 4.9. Scene produced by an early GE visual simulator built for NASA. (Provided by Lew DeWitt.)

Fading is implemented by employing two variable-gain amplifiers, called A and B (Figure 4.11). The inputs to amplifier A are a video signal S_A and a fading value F. The inputs to amplifier B are a signal S_B and a value $(1 - F)$. Video signals S_A and S_B are functions of the modulo 2 sums of the four component texture values. Let

$$
\begin{aligned}
S_1 &= T_1 \oplus T_2 \oplus T_3 \oplus T_4 \\
S_2 &= T_2 \oplus T_3 \oplus T_4 \\
S_3 &= T_3 \oplus T_4 \\
S_4 &= T_4
\end{aligned}
$$

In zone 1, $S_A = S_1$ is applied to amplifier A with a gain of F, and $S_B = S_2$ is applied to amplifier B with a gain of $(1 - F)$. As F decreases, amplifier A's gain decreases and amplifier B's gain increases. The result is a video signal in which the contribution of T_1 gradually decreases with increasing slant range. In zone 2, $S_A = S_3$ is applied to amplifier A and $S_B = S_2$ is applied to amplifier B. The T_2 component fades as F increases. The operations performed in each of the six slant-range zones are tabulated in Figure 4.12.

The night-sky pattern of stars is also treated as a texture. A sky texture is placed on a plane at a fixed height above the ground. To make the

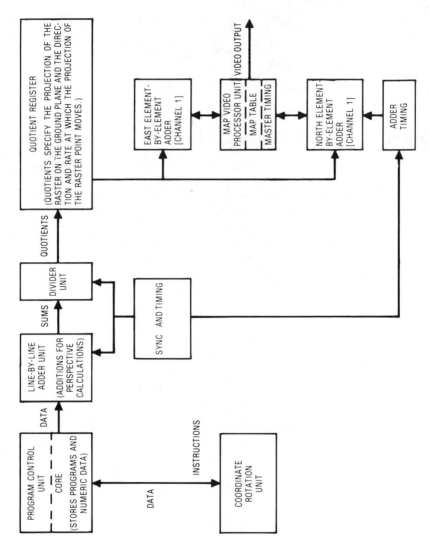

Figure 4.10. Block diagram of GE NASA three-view space flight simulator.

63

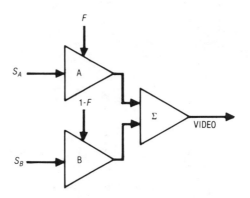

Figure 4.11. Variable-gain amplifiers used for texture component fading.

HORIZON	ZONE	AMPLIFIER A		AMPLIFIER B	
		INPUT	GAIN	INPUT	GAIN
	5	BC	DON'T CARE	BC	DON'T CARE
	4	BC		S_4	
	3	S_3		S_4	
	2	S_3		S_2	
	1	S_1		S_2	
	0	S_1	DON'T CARE	S_1	DON'T CARE

SLANT RANGE

VIEWPOINT

1   F   0   1-F

Figure 4.12. Summary of inputs to amplifiers A and B. (BC denotes the background color intensity of the horizon.)

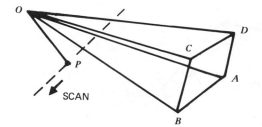

Figure 4.13. Illustration of the relationship between the viewpoint and the vertices of face F.

pattern appear to be at near infinity, the night-sky texture does not respond to the simulated vehicle's translation.

The raster structure is identical to that of normal commercial TV, utilizing 525 lines with a 2:1 interlace and a 30 frame per second update rate. However, instead of supplying normal horizontal and vertical sweep to the deflection yoke, a composite waveform is applied, which is a function of the vehicle's roll.

Later versions of this simulator have the ability to display a limited number of objects. A 1966 report [GE66] describes a unit which can display two rectilinearly oriented parallelepipeds standing on level ground. Back-facing faces of the objects are eliminated from consideration by computing the dot product of the current view ray and surface normals. If the view ray passes through the remaining portion of an object, it must pass through one or more of the top-, bottom-, or front-facing faces. These conditions are denoted by the logic variables T, B, and F. $\bar{T} \cap \bar{B} \cap \bar{F}$ describes the condition when a view ray does not intersect the object.

Let the vertices of a front-facing face of an object be denoted by A, B, C, and D (Figure 4.13). A view ray starts at the viewpoint O, passes through the current raster scan point P, and on into the 3-D environment. In order to determine whether a view ray passes through face $ABCD$, it is determined whether the view ray passes simultaneously above line AB, to the left of BC, below CD, and to the right of DA. These four conditions are specified by the logic variables F_1, F_2, F_3, and F_4, respectively:

$$F_1 = \text{True if and only if } \mathbf{OP} \cdot \mathbf{OA} \times \mathbf{OB} < 0$$
$$F_2 = \text{True if and only if } \mathbf{OP} \cdot \mathbf{OB} \times \mathbf{OC} < 0$$
$$F_3 = \text{True if and only if } \mathbf{OP} \cdot \mathbf{OC} \times \mathbf{OD} < 0$$
$$F_4 = \text{True if and only if } \mathbf{OP} \cdot \mathbf{OD} \times \mathbf{OA} < 0$$

Thus the condition that the view ray passes through $ABCD$ is $F = F_1 \cap F_2 \cap F_3 \cap F_4$. Consider line AB. To determine on which side of AB the

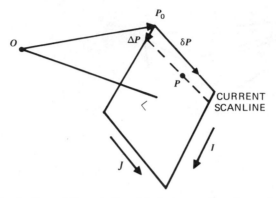

Figure 4.14.   Illustration of the relationship between the viewpoint and the raster scan point.

view ray passes, the sign of $Q = \mathbf{OP} \cdot \mathbf{OA} \times \mathbf{OB}$ is monitored. The vector **OP** can be expanded into a row and column sum by the equation

$$\mathbf{OP} = \mathbf{OP_0} + \Delta P \mathbf{I} + \delta P \mathbf{J}$$

where ΔP and δP are the screen components of P, and **I** and **J** are unit vectors in the I and J directions (Figure 4.14). $\mathbf{OP_0}$ is the vector joining the viewpoint to the top left screen point. We can write

$$\begin{aligned} Q &= \mathbf{OP_0} \cdot \mathbf{OA} \times \mathbf{OP} + \Delta P \mathbf{I} \, \mathbf{OA} \times \mathbf{OB} + \delta P \mathbf{J} \, \mathbf{OA} \times \mathbf{OB} \\ &= Q_0 + \Delta Q + \delta Q \end{aligned}$$

A hardware module called an obstacle side generator continually monitors the sign of Q for each of the edges in the data base. Logic operations on the resultant information yield the raster scan conversion of the objects.

Since a view ray may intersect more than one face, hidden-surface elimination must still be performed. This is accomplished by determining the relationship between the viewpoint and the faces of the object. For example, the top faces have priority over side faces, except when the viewpoint is below the top. Both objects have priority over the ground plane. Priority between the two objects is determined by the relationship between the viewpoint and a plane separating the objects.

Later versions of this device can display slightly more complex objects. The resultant scene is still rather primitive, as seen in Figure 4.15.

4.2.1.2. GE ASUPT System [BEAR77]

The ASUPT system (now called ASPT) consists of three major hardware units (Figure 4.16): general-purpose computers (frame I), special-purpose computers (frame II), and raster scan conversion and CRT electronics (frame III). The three computation units are connected serially to form a pipeline processor with a $\frac{3}{30}$-second throughput delay.

Frame I is built around two general-purpose central processor units (CPU A and CPU B). CPU A performs arithmetic operations and "talks" to the flight computer. CPU B handles certain management tasks, including the search and retrieval of data blocks from the visual data-base disk. These blocks describe the new geographic regions which the pilot encounters. CPU B has 8K of core to itself; it shares two 8K core modules with CPU A. All data sent to the special-purpose computer are first loaded into one of the two shared memory modules.

Frame I receives the aircraft's instantaneous position and attitude from the flight computer. Frame I also does some preliminary processing, such as slant range to model centroid tests, to determine the correct level of detail at which to display models. (A model is defined by GE as any collection of object faces for which relative priorities have been determined and stored during off-line data-base development.) Frame I also performs some data-base culling. Objects completely outside the field of view are eliminated. Since geometric and video processing must be performed differently for each display channel, objects are placed into groups according to the display channel for which they may be visible. This process is called channel assignment. It is accomplished by enclosing each object in a sphere and determining which spheres fall entirely or partially into the pyramidal view cones of the individual channels. The channel-assignment operation is achieved with the help of the vector-processing hardware of frame II.

The data calculated in frame I are sent to frame II via a bidirectional frame I/frame II interface. The on-line environmental data storage memories of frame II are updated by CPU B from data temporarily kept in its memory module.

Frame II is principally a vector-processing computer. Every vertex of every potentially visible object is specified either in the environment's fixed coordinate system or in a moving coordinate system. The viewpoint is assigned a moving coordinate system, since it moves through the environment. The vertices and edges making up the 3-D scene are projected onto each view window each frame time. Each moving model, such as an

Figure 4.15. Several scenes produced by a late-model GE visual simulator built for NASA.

(c)

Figure 4.15.   (continued)

aircraft flying through the environment, is assigned its own moving coordinate system. A set of vectors, joining the viewpoint and vertices of each moving model, is computed each frame time.

The frame II edge processor (pipeline) converts channel-specific viewpoint data into a stream of object- and channel-specific edges. The pipeline processes the edges of each object in sequence. Leaving the pipeline are data describing the projections of edges on the view windows. When Gouraud continuous shading is used, special face-oriented processing of objects takes place. This is accomplished by passing an object through the pipeline twice, computing continuous shading data in the first pass and doing normal edge processing in the second.

Hidden-surface elimination is accomplished using the priority-list approach. A priority processor constructs a list containing a unique priority number for each face, based upon viewpoint, active data lists, and separation plane and relative priority data obtained from the data base. The stages of operation are as follows. Viewpoint and moving model positions are received from frame I at the start of each raster period. Using these data, the priority processor establishes the relative priorities of the coordinate systems, producing a top-level priority list containing a single entry for each coordinate system. Then, for each entry in the top-level priority list, the priority processor constructs a priority list with a single entry for each model of each coordinate system. A complete model priority list is created by combining the individual coordinate system model priority lists, using the relative order of coordinate system priorities.

Next, the priority processor creates a separate priority list for each active model. These lists have a single entry for each object of a model.

In the final stage, the individual object priority lists are combined in model priority list order to obtain a complete active-object priority list. The priority numbers of ground plane faces are then combined with the

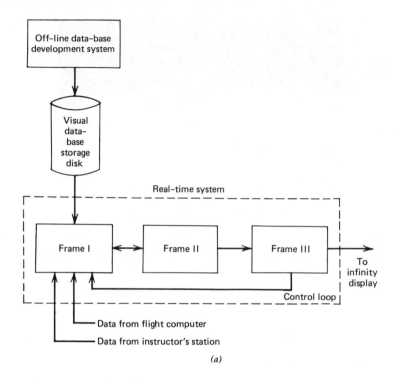

Real-time system

To infinity display

Control loop

Data from flight computer

Data from instructor's station

(a)

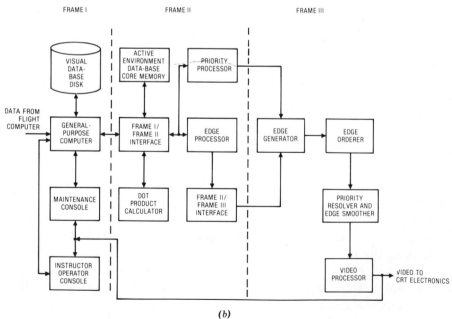

(b)

Figure 4.16. (a) GE ASUPT system configuration. (b) ASUPT CIG system; functional diagram. (From [BEAR77]).

priority numbers of object faces to form the final list. Because the lower 4 bits of the priority number are reserved for ground faces and the upper 4 bits are reserved for object faces, objects always have priority over the planar ground surface.

The frame II/frame III interface accepts edge words from the frame II edge processor in arbitrary sequence, provides temporary storage for the edge words, determines the proper sequence for the edge words associated with an object, and transfers these data to the frame III edge buffer storage.

The edge generator computes the intersection of each edge with each scan line that crosses it. The edge generator can handle a maximum of 256 edges per scan line per channel (a maximum of 2560 potentially visible edges per channel). First, the J value of the intersection of an edge with the uppermost scan line crossing it is computed. The slope of the edge is specified in terms of elements per scan line. The intersection of the edge with each succeeding scan line is accomplished by simply adding this slope to the previous J value. (The details of implementation are complicated by the $2:1$ interlaced scanout used. We ignore complications resulting from the interlacing scheme for the sake of understandability.) The output of the edge generator is a sequence of J values along with their edge identifications.

The edge orderer receives edge crossings for each scan line. These J values are not yet ordered across a scan line, except that the values resulting from the same object are in order. The edge orderer sorts the edge-crossing values by scan-element number. These ordered edge data are then placed into an ordered-data memory.

Final hidden-surface calculations are performed by a priority resolver, which receives priority lists from frame II and edge data from the ordered-data memory. Priority resolution is essentially a convex-object-oriented function. When the left element of an object is received for a channel, the object identification is entered in a list. When the right edge of an object is received, the object identification is removed. Thus at any moment, the priority list contains the identities of all objects pierced by a ray from the viewpoint, through the raster element being computed, into the 3-D environment. The priority resolver uses the available priority information to determine which of these pierced faces is closest to the viewpoint. This determination holds for succeeding raster elements along a scan line, until there is a change in the list. The output of the priority resolver is divided among the display channels and sent to the frame III video processor for each display channel.

ASUPT has a total of 14 video processors, divided among two cockpits, seven channels per cockpit. Each video processor receives one line of data at a time from the priority resolver. A video processor outputs one scan line at a time in synchrony with the TV raster scanout. Edge smoothing is performed in frame III partially by the video processors and partially by the priority resolver. The priority resolver calculates the position of an edge within a raster element. A video processor uses an area-times-gray-level algorithm to calculate an intensity assignment for the pixel. This calculation is not exact. At most, only the values of the faces of highest priority to the left and right of an edge, plus a background value, are combined. During the last stage of video processing, the computed 10-bit gray shade of each pixel along a scan line is converted to analog by a high-speed D/A converter.

4.2.1.3. GE C-130 Visual Simulator

GE's fourth-generation systems are the most advanced ever built. Since their algorithmic structure is similar to that of the company's third-generation products, the discussion that follows will only emphasize the differences.

The C-130 frame I hardware consists of a 32-bit general-purpose computer and the usual peripherals [SCHA80b]. The frame I software mainly performs data management, monitoring, and control tasks. It retrieves data blocks from disk to describe each new geographic region the pilot encounters.

In third-generation GE systems, frame II processing is performed by hardwired pipeline processors. If new computations are desired, new hardware must be designed. GE's fourth-generation systems use non-dedicated programmable pipeline processors (Figure 4.17). If additional algorithms must be implemented, it is only necessary to add identical units and program them as required. The programming and controlling of a number of pipeline processors running in parallel—to keep them all continuously operating at maximum efficiency with a minimum of time spent on overhead tasks such as data and control transfers—is of course no easy task. This topic is just beginning to be discussed in the computer literature [KART80].

C-130's frame II consists of a controller, a priority processor, a bank of nondedicated programmable pipeline processors, and an active environment core storage unit. Frame II receives blocks of environmental data from frame I and places them in core. Generic 3-D models also reside on line in core. The active-environment memory contains all the information required to construct a scene. Frame II uses these data to build a new 2-D image for each display channel each raster period. The frame II controller

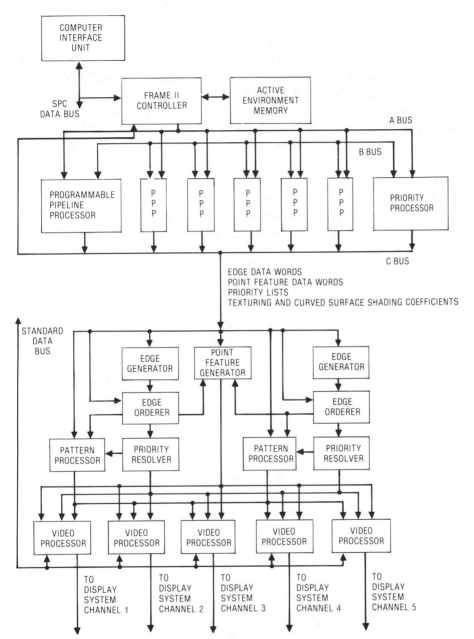

Figure 4.17. Block diagram of frames II and III of a typical GE 5-channel fourth-generation visual system.

uses a distributed approach to control authority. Each control processor is a fixed program sequencer designed to support a particular function with a minimum of external interaction. The functions that are controlled include environment update, collision detection, data processing, bus interface, vector processing, and active face, block, cluster, and region assignment. The operation of each sequencer is basically asynchronous, with data and control transfers handled by a pseudo-FIFO memory structure. This allows each sequencer to run at the maximum possible rate while minimizing critical timing interrelationships.

Frame II sends frame III point, edge, face, priority, and texture data words at each frame time. Frame III uses this information to construct a recognizable image in raster format. A number of hardware modules are responsible for this function. For each active scan line, an edge generator determines which edges intersect the line (actually treated as a strip), calculates the points of edge intersection with the top and bottom of the line (strip), and outputs the resulting intercept values and edge numbers to an edge orderer. Over 600 edge crossings and 300 light point crossings per scan line can be handled. The edge orderer orders edge crossings along a scan line first by channel and then within a channel by element number. The edge orderer also obtains the stored data associated with each edge and sends them to a priority resolver. The priority resolver arbitrates priority conflicts, calculates edge smoothing area weighting coefficients, and outputs visible edge data to the video processors. (While ASUPT performed edge smoothing in the horizontal direction only, C-130 performs 2-D geometric edge smoothing.) Each high-speed video processor also receives point and texture data from the point source generator and pattern processors, respectively. The texture generators, located within the video processors, produce 15 different textures, each at ten levels of detail, with blending between successive levels of detail [BUNK77c, SCHA80a, SCHA80c]. One video processor is required to feed each window of the simulator. These video processors each compute picture element colors (12 bits red, 12 bits green, 12 bits blue) at a rate of 30×10^6 pixels per second.

The special-purpose hardware in frames II and III is built from over 1.4×10^5 integrated circuits. These include MSI and SSI TTL chips for logic and control and 4000-bit LSI chips for memory. A scene from the GE C-130 device is shown in Figure 4.18.

4.2.2. Singer Company, Link Division

Link pilot training devices have been manufactured since 1929. Singer/Link began introducing devices with CIG capability in the mid 1970s.

Figure 4.18.   Scene produced by GE C-130 visual simulator.

Several Singer/Link dusk/night systems are described in Section 4.2.2.1 followed by two day/dusk/night systems in Section 4.2.2.2.

4.2.2.1.   *Link Night Visual System (NVS) and Link-Miles Image II System*

NVS is a low-cost simulator attachment for generating night scenes [CHEN75]. NVS can display 2000 to 6000 light points at a 30 frame per second update rate. The first stage of the system is a PDP-11 minicomputer (Figure 4.19). The light point data base is stored in the minicomputer's core. The minicomputer obtains owncraft (the pilot's own craft's) position and attitude from the host flight computer and sends these and light point data to a bank of image processors. The image processors calculate vectors joining the viewpoint and each light point, rotate these 3-D vectors to place the light points into the appropriate aircraft window axes, project these light points onto the display windows, and clip light points falling outside the field of view. The colors, intensities, and 2-D positions of light points are sent to image generators. Each independent display channel has its own image generator. The image generators receive weather data from the instructor station via the interface and control

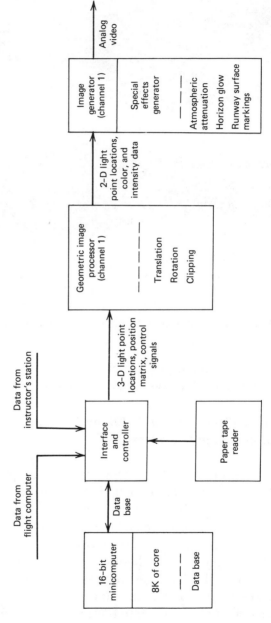

Figure 4.19. Block diagram of an early Singer/Link NVS.

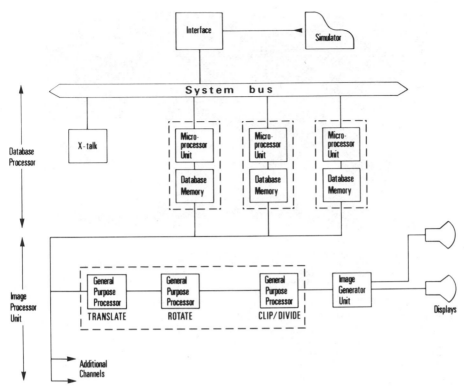

Figure 4.20.   Block diagram of Link-Miles Image II visual system.

unit. Each image generator contains a special effects generator to add horizon glow, runway tire markings, and atmospheric attenuation. The image generators output analog video to drive beam penetration tubes. Four possible colors (yellow-white, red, orange, and green) are written over 4096 × 4096 addressable points. An infinity imaging system consisting of spherical mirrors and beam splitters produces a rather narrow field of view in the standard configuration. NVS devices are known for their excellent 3-D realism. A pilot can "fly" over, under, and through points of light suspended in the atmosphere.

The Link-Miles Division of the Singer Company (U.K.) Limited has designed a dusk/night visual system, called Image II. The system is unusual in that the first stage of processing is handled by three Intel 8086/8087 single-board computers in parallel (Figure 4.20). Three Image II units are scheduled to be delivered to the U.S. Air Force's new training center in Pittsburgh in 1983. Two scenes produced by Image II can be seen in Figure 4.21. A day/night visual system, called Image III, is now in its final stages of development.

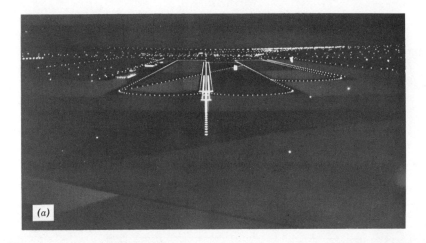

Figure 4.21.   Two scenes produced by Link-Miles Image II visual system.

4.2.2.2.   *Singer/Link Digital Image Generation (DIG) System*

Singer/Link has two generations of DIG machines. The first is rated at 8000 edges at a 30 frame per second update rate. It has been delivered in a variety of configurations to NASA Johnson Space Center, the U.S. Air Force, Northrop Aircraft, All Nippon Airways, the U.S. Army, and NASA Ames. The first-generation machine is covered first, followed by a description of the improvements which transform it into a second-generation model.

Singer/Link calls the 32-bit general-purpose computer at the front end

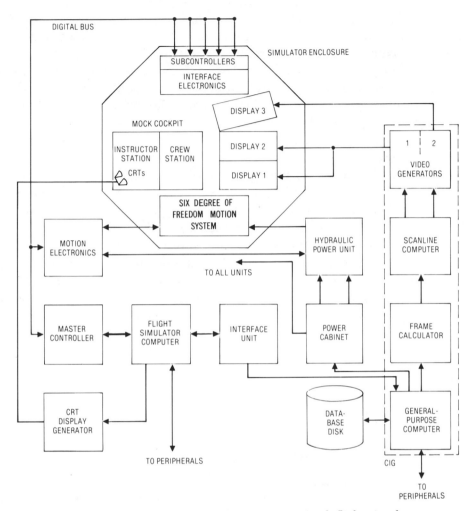

Figure 4.22.   Block diagram of entire Singer/Link flight simulator.

of its system (Figure 4.22) a digital image generation controller (DIGC). It has 384K of private core and supports the usual peripherals. The DIGC accepts owncraft heading, position, attitude, rate of attitude change, velocity, weather conditions, and other data from the flight computer. From these inputs, the DIGC dynamically extracts object descriptions from disk and places them in an active data base (ADB) memory. The ADB is that portion of the total data base which is within the vicinity of the aircraft at any point in time. The DIGC also computes occultation priorities, controls the allocation of ADB memory, and directs the activities of the image-generation hardware.

The DIGC's software modules fall into three categories: extrapolation, synchronous, and asynchronous. Extrapolation modules execute as high-priority foreground tasks to determine the position and attitude of own-craft and all moving scene components each frame time. This requires an extrapolation of the input data, which are not necessarily synchronized with the image generator's frame rate. Synchronous modules compute other data as required by the image-generation hardware. Asynchronous modules run as background tasks, performing less urgent functions such as data retrieval and priority calculations.

Data bases are organized into area blocks of, typically, either 10.8 × 10.8 or 5.4 × 5.4 square miles. A commercial airline data base usually covers a region of 80 × 80 square nautical miles. A military data base may be as large as several hundred miles in each dimension. Data are retrieved from disk in the form of either area records or cluster records. An area record contains no object descriptions, but rather identifies the clusters of objects within an area block. The DIGC identifies the area block directly below owncraft and retrieves from disk all area block records within a square centered about this particular block. Singer calls this square terrain region a panorama (Figure 4.23). The chosen panorama size is a function of mission visibility conditions.

Each cluster in the panorama is tested to determine whether any por-

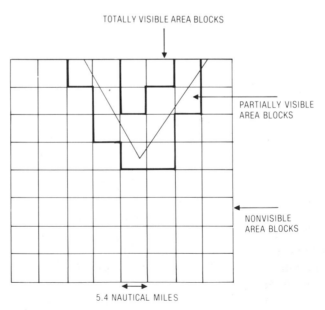

Figure 4.23. Potentially visible area blocks within panorama.

tion of it is potentially visible. A pyramid of vision slightly larger than the field of view is used to prevent lags during attitude changes. A code is assigned to each cluster to indicate whether it is in view, out of view, or partially in view.

The level of detail at which a cluster is retrieved is based upon the distance between the viewpoint and the cluster's centroid and on switching-range values stored with the cluster. By allowing switching ranges for successive levels of detail to overlap slightly, frequent switching between two levels of detail is prevented.

The priority-list approach is used to solve the hidden-surface problem. Certain priorities are computed in advance and stored on the visual database disk. Separation plane data are also stored on the disk in binary tree form [SCHN76, BENN75] (Figure 4.24). The nodes of the tree represent separating planes, and the leaves represent convex objects. The relative priorities of objects that have not been previously specified are determined by the DIGC on a block-by-block basis. Relative object priorities within a block are determined by searching the separating plane tree. This approach is also used for airborne clusters by placing separating planes below the clusters. Finally, relative priorities are converted into absolute priorities by using the relationships among the area blocks. This process uses the observation that an object in a far block cannot obscure an object in a nearer block (Figure 4.25).

The DIGC is connected to the image-generation hardware through three direct memory access channels (Figure 4.26). The ADB is transferred to the ADB memory through one of these channels. Geometric processing is under software control through the second channel. For every frame, positions and attitude of owncraft and all moving objects are transferred to a frame calculator, followed by a list of objects to be processed for each video channel. The third direct memory access channel is used to transfer color codes, computation parameters, and hardware diagnostic information.

The frame calculator is arranged into a pipeline composed of an object processor, a face visibility tester, a rotation and illumination subsystem, a clipper, and a face boundary calculator. The object processor examines every object in the list received from the DIGC and eliminates all back-facing faces. All faces that are very small in projection are eliminated by a face-visibility test which is under dynamic control. Part of the object processor's task is to transform pilot position into object coordinate systems. The resultant vertices are passed to the rotation and illumination subsystem together with a list of front-facing faces. The rotation and illumination subsystem transforms vertices of faces into window coordi-

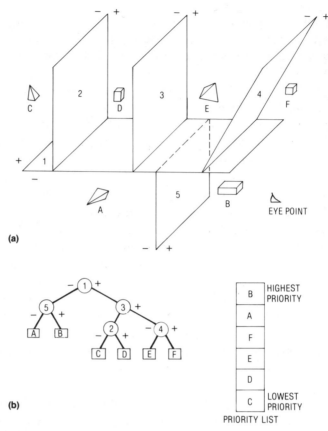

Figure 4.24. (a) Relationship between objects, separating planes, and eyepoint. (The − and + signs refer to the dot product of the view vector on the surface normals of the separating planes.) (From [BENN75].) (b) Separating plane tree.

6	5	4	3	4
4	3	2	3	
3	2	1		
	1	0		

VIEW DIRECTION

Figure 4.25. Relative area block priorities. Here, 0 denotes the highest priority.

82

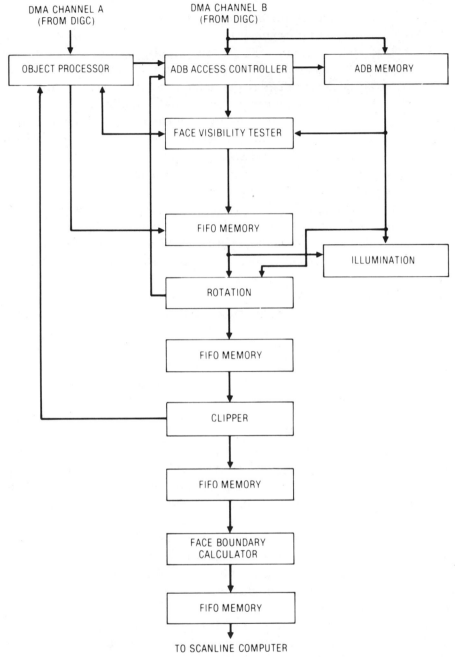

Figure 4.26. Frame calculator block diagram.

83

nates and in parallel determines the illumination for each face. These data are passed on to the clipping subsystem, which uses Singer's own version of Sutherland and Hodgman's [SUTH74b] clipping algorithm.

The boundary calculator receives sequences of vertices defining faces. It calculates all necessary display parameters in view plane coordinates. The first section of the boundary calculator is a pipeline processor that projects vertices onto the view windows. Divisions are performed in the logarithm domain, using a logarithm lookup table, a subtractor, and an antilog lookup table. The second section of the boundary calculator is a parallel group of processors that convert vertices into view plane edges. Edge data consist of the (I, J) location, intensities, and fading values at the endpoints of each edge. The third section of the boundary calculator is a pipeline processor which computes the rate of change (along an edge) of J coordinates, intensity, and fading coefficients. Intensity and fading rates of changes across scan lines are also computed. Divisions are carried out in the logarithm domain.

Between the frame calculator and the scan-line computer is a double buffer memory to hold two edge lists of 8000 edges each. Geometric data produced by the frame calculator are written into one edge buffer. At the same time, data produced by the frame calculator during the previous frame time are read out of the other edge buffer and into the scan-line computer. When the frame calculator and the scan-line computer have completed processing a frame's worth of data, the two sections of memory are switched for the next frame time's processing. This type of memory switching is sometimes called ping-ponging.

The scan-line computer (Figure 4.27) consists of a sort and update subsystem, occulting logic, and video generator arranged into a pipeline.

Data coming out of the edge buffer memory pass through the update logic. There the starting parameters are updated according to the interlaced field that is being processed. The updated edge data enter the sort logic where up to 256 edges per scan line are ordered by J value. The sort is accomplished by two passes through a pipeline. The sorted J values, along with other data, are sent to the occulting subsystem. Sorted edge data are also fed back to the update logic, where they are used in processing the next scan line in the same field.

The occulting logic computes the visibility at intersections and determines the intensities of partially obscured surfaces at the points at which they become visible. Visibility is determined by examining edge intersections within a scan line, in sequence, and creating an "active object" list. An object is placed into the list when its leftmost edge is encountered and removed when its rightmost edge is reached. A temporary memory holds

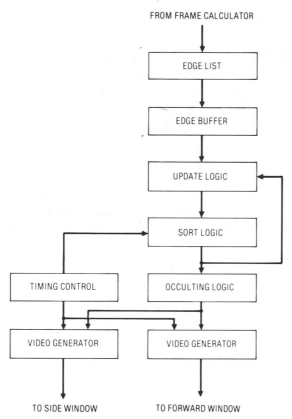

Figure 4.27.   Scanline computer block diagram.

the intensity associated with the last encountered intersection of an object, along with the intensity increment and color code to its right. The face associated with an intersection point is visible if it results from an object whose priority is highest in the active object list. If the intersection point results from a beginning or internal edge, the intensity at that point is determined by the intensity value associated with that edge. If an intersection point results from an ending edge of a visible object, the intensity assignment is taken from the next highest priority object in the active object list (meaning that the left portion of this next highest priority object is obscured). The last encountered intensity parameters of this partially obscured object are retrieved from temporary memory. The correct intensity value is then computed for the particular location along the scan line at which the partially obscured object becomes visible. The output of the occulting logic is a compressed description of the color along a scan line. It is in the form of a sequence of visible intersections, their associated intensity values, the intensity increments for faces to their right, and color codes.

Singer/Link permits a special type of face called a level-of-detail face. The intensity of the level-of-detail face is blended to the intensity of the underlying face in the occult subsystem. Incremental intensity is computed as a function of face size on the screen calculated by the frame calculator, thereby permitting gradual and graceful introduction of scene detail.

The scan-line computer processes the data for each scan line serially, one channel at a time. For each channel, the processed data for one scan line are stored in a buffer memory. This permits simultaneous scan-line output for the channels to separate video generators. At the same time, data for the next scan line for each channel are being computed and stored.

A video generator (Figure 4.28) computes intensity and fading across a

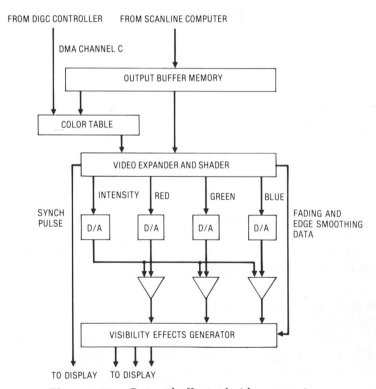

Figure 4.28.   Output buffer and video generator.

surface using incremental values. This expanded pixel description is then converted into 8 bits each of red, green, and blue for each point along a scan line. This is done by using a lookup table to convert the color codes into color components. An intensity value and the red, green, and blue color components are fed into four fast D/A converters to provide three video signals. Finally, these red, green, and blue signals are modified by fading and by horizontal and vertical edge smoothing.*

Singer/Link offers a landing-light option, which brightens scene components within landing-light or taxi-light lobes. The lobe shape is stored in tables loaded from the DIGC.

A Singer/Link second-generation DIG unit has been built for the B-52 aircraft. The frame calculator has been changed to include a "bubble test" for objects. Each object is enclosed within a sphere, which is checked for inclusion within the view pyramids. The frame calculator has been streamlined to permit a significant throughput increase: 12,000 edges or points at 30 Hz or 6000 at 60 Hz. The data base can now be up to six times larger than that for previous systems. The edge-list buffer has been expanded to accommodate the increased processing capacity of the frame calculator. The scan-line computer can now handle 512 intersections per scan line. The permitted number of explicit priorities has been increased to 1024 per channel. The scan-line computer now also permits the computation of up to four subscan lines for antialiasing; this is accomplished by performing an incremental update of the subscan lines and another J sort. Parameters for multisurface averaging within a pixel are generated in the scan-line computer. The averaging required for edges vertical to the scan line is performed in the occult subsystem, while that for other edges is performed in the video generators.

Illumination calculations now can also accommodate infrared emissivities by using a table (loaded by the DIGC) containing material emissivities and time lags. Other sensor types, such as low-light-level television (LLLTV), can also be simulated.

Figures 4.29 and 4.30 show two photographs taken from Singer/Link's latest operational equipment. The first photograph shows Tokyo's Hanada airport as presented on a system delivered to All Nippon Airways. The second photograph contains an out-the-window scene taken from the B-52 system. This photograph also shows an LLLTV display, which is driven from the same image generator that produced the visuals.

---

*Singer uses the term horizontal (vertical) edge smoothing to refer to the smoothing of edges less (greater) than 45° with respect to scan-line rows.

Figure 4.29. A photograph taken from Singer/Link's visual system delivered to All Nippon Airways. (This photograph is reproduced in color in the color section.)

Figure 4.30. A photograph taken from Singer/Link's B-52 visual system.

4.2.3.   Evans and Sutherland Computer Company (E&S)/Rediffusion, Ltd.

E&S is a high-technology computer graphics company founded in 1968 by two well-known computer scientists, David Evans and Ivan Sutherland. All design and manufacturing facilities are located at the University of Utah Research Park in Salt Lake City. The company offers only two categories of products, interactive graphics systems and flight simulator visuals. E&S's sale of CIG devices is exclusively to Rediffusion, which usually builds the simulation facility, combines it with E&S's visual system, and markets the entire package. Their two main simulator products are reviewed below.

4.2.3.1.   NOVOVIEW

The first NOVOVIEW device was delivered in 1973. It is a low-cost, real-time, night-only system. It generates perspective scenes containing up to 2000 light points and a shaded horizon band. Soon after the introduction of NOVOVIEW, E&S realized that their simulators required a richer scene content.

NOVOVIEW was improved in 1974 to display a runway surface and markings, and to generate over 2500 light points. In 1975 the capability was expanded to display over 6000 (red, green, white, and orange) lights with excellent clarity and resolution. These light points are effectively used to create a detailed airport complex, but are sparse elsewhere. NOVOVIEW's standard display configuration produces a narrow vertical field of view which allows straight ahead tasks, but makes attitude control difficult at pitch angles greater than 10° up. The horizon is outside the field of view in the side windows at bank angles of 15° or greater, making it difficult for the pilot to maneuver the aircraft. Some models of this type effectively display such special effects as stars, moon, an aura surrounding the airport, and a glowing sunrise/sunset. The year 1976 saw improvements in weather effects and the simulation of the illumination due to landing lights. These improvements can be retrofitted into earlier NOVOVIEW devices.

NOVOVIEW SP1 was introduced in 1977. It provides increased surface capacity (200 surfaces), solid and moving objects, directional lights, and a dusk mode capability. NOVOVIEW SP2 differs from the SP1 device in that it uses a shadow-mask CRT. Lights are simulated by directing the electron beam to the proper point on the CRT, and turning it on with the proper color. A linear deflection system is used to paint a full 800-line

Figure 4.31. Scenes produced by Evans and Sutherland image generators. (Part d appears in color in the color section.)

raster, with all surfaces displayed in a raster scan mode. The raster is rotated in real time to be parallel to the horizon. Image brightness is carefully controlled to eliminate flicker. Day, dusk, and night scenes of moderate complexity (450 surfaces) are produced (Figure 4.31a,b,c). The 3-D objects are displayed at varying levels of detail. The update rate is 40 frames per second for the daylight mode and 30 frames per second for the night mode. System overload conditions are handled by reducing the update rate. If the update rate reaches some lower bound, fewer scan lines are computed, with the surviving scan lines spread out. This allows for increased processing time per scan line.

4.2.3.2.   E&S's Continuous-Tone Systems

E&S's continuous-tone devices are higher cost image generators that emphasize scene quality. A raster scan approach is used to display the entire scene content. The first unit of this type (CT-1) was delivered to Case Western Reserve University in 1973. It uses a high-precision monochromatic CRT camera station to produce animated color movies in non-real time by sequencing color filters. The speed of the system is a function of the complexity of the scenes being generated. Scenes can contain up to

400 polygons. Gouraud continuous shading and edge smoothing are employed.

A CIG device was delivered in 1975 to the Computer Aided Operations Research Facility of the National Maritime Research Center. The system simulates the views required for such shipboard operations as open-sea navigation, harbor piloting, and docking. The components of the scene include navigation aids such as buoys, shoreline, bridges, buildings, docks, ships, and various kinds of lights. Up to 1200 polygons are displayed simultaneously. The display covers a 240° field of view in azimuth and 24° in elevation. Five color Eidiphor TV projectors display the imagery in a color/field sequential mode.

A higher performance device called an electronic scene generator was delivered to the Johnson Space Center in 1976. This device is mainly used to study the design of the cargo-handling system of the space shuttle. Two separate images are generated, depicting scenes viewable from zoom cameras mounted on the shuttle manipulator, around the cargo bay area, or out the window. The image generator can process about 900 polygons.

Two CT-4 image generators were delivered to Lufthansa in 1977. These devices can display 400 polygons and 4000 light points. Polygons are selected for processing only if their projected size on the display exceeds a given area threshold. When an overload condition is anticipated, a data management program running in the controlling general-purpose computer raises the acceptance threshold. A very-high-quality picture is obtained by sampling the image at four subscan lines and as many subelements within each pixel, by state-of-the-art edge smoothing, and by a field update rate (50 Hz) of the image (Figure 4.31d). Lights are subjected to sophisticated filtering and raster scan conversion processing to assure the preservation of their size, shape, and brightness as they move about the raster.

E&S is a subcontractor to Reflectone, Inc., on two 6-channel CIG modules (called CT-5) for use in Reflectone's Ch-46E helicopter trainer. These units display 2500 polygons at a field update rate. The trainer is designed for the twin-turbine tandem-rotor helicopters of the U.S. Marine Corps, manufactured by Boeing Vertol Company. The instructor sits in a control station and can "fly" as a pilot or copilot, with limited control over the training session. The last 5 minutes of operation are recorded on tape for playback, with the accompanying instructor's voice commentary. The following types of training missions will be practiced with the simulator: confined area takeoffs and landings, shipboard takeoffs and landings, inclement weather operations, sling load operation, and formation flying.

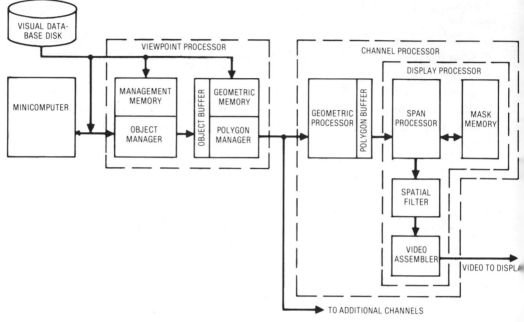

Figure 4.32.   Block diagram of Evans and Sutherland CT-5 visual system.

The first stage of the CT-5 is a minicomputer which performs such tasks as data-base retrieval and overload management (Figure 4.32) [SCHU80].

The second stage is a viewpoint processor which consists of an object manager, a polygon manager, and two independent memories. The viewpoint processor performs tasks specific to the momentary viewpoint rather than to any particular view window. It executes various data-base culling operations, including field-of-view inclusion and rejection of back-facing faces and faces smaller than the allowed threshold. The viewpoint processor feeds a geometric processor which performs view-window-specific computations including rotation, clipping, and perspective divisions. The resultant image-plane data for a channel are stored in a dual polygon buffer. The buffer contains view window descriptions of polygons and/or lights. Scene components are arranged in priority order. While one side of this dual memory is being written into at a field rate (normally), a complete scene's worth of data (i.e., both fields) is being read from the other side.

The polygon buffer supplies 2-D geometric data to a display processor. The display processor receives and processes scene components in priority order. Thus scene components received earlier will occult later ones. The display processor consists of a span processor, a mask memory, a spatial filter, and a video assembler. It performs hidden-surface elimination, antialiasing, and raster scan conversion. The CT-5 system is the first raster scan CIG device built by an established company in the business which does not use a scan-line approach to scene generation. Images are computed in feature sequential order rather than in scan-line order. Area representations are the basic units for processing, rather than scan-line samples.

The processing hardware is organized into units which operate in parallel on regions of the display, called spans. A span is a cell of a rectangular tessellation of the view window (Figure 4.33). Each span, in effect, represents an array of pixels. Individual scene components, such as polygons, are processed in span-sized chunks. The algorithms which do the processing for a span operate on analytic descriptions of scene components rather than on sampled versions of them. The processing time for a span is essentially unrelated to the complexity of the scene geometry within it. Only when the number of edges in a scene component contained in a single span gets large does the processing time increase beyond the nominal value for that span. The time to process an entire scene depends principally on the number of spans intersecting partially or wholly visible scene elements. Completely hidden scene components are bypassed at minimal cost. This results in a processing cost that is much better than linear. Measurements on the real-time hardware have demonstrated that the displayed image's complexity can be doubled with less than a 25 percent increase in the computational load. E&S sees this as an encouraging sign that system size may remain manageable with arbitrary growth in scene content.

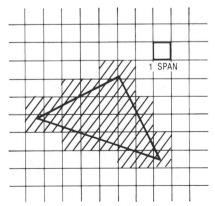

Figure 4.33. Illustration of a polygon intersecting an array of spans. The cross-hatched region is the total span area which must be processed for the polygon.

A mask memory stores a high-resolution composite record of all scene components processed thus far for a field. Only information indicating the existence or absence of scene data is stored. When a polygon is submitted to the span processor, an analytic description is formed of the portion of the polygon covered by the span. A description of image regions already processed for the span is obtained from the mask memory. The new polygon, minus the higher priority mask area, is passed to a spatial filter. The inclusive OR of the new polygon with the mask becomes the new contents of the mask memory.

The spatial filter consists of a set of identical filters, one for each pixel in a span. Each pixel-centered filter convolves a generally circularly symmetric function of nonuniform weights with the surrounding scene elements. The filter unit not only implements edge smoothing, but it also handles such effects as smooth shading, fading, color blending, and translucency.

The spatial filter feeds span-size arrays of video, in parallel, to a video assembler. The video assembler is a dual buffer with storage for the red, green, and blue components of an image at display resolution. While the ping side of this buffer is supplying video to a display, the pong side is accepting scene data for the next field.

A number of common approaches to overload management are applied in combination. The size threshold for accepting faces is dynamically adjusted to control the number of polygons passing through the pipeline. The level-of-detail selection parameters and the ranges at which switching occurs are also adjusted when necessary. If conditions deteriorate so rapidly that the hardware units cannot complete their tasks in the allocated time, the field rate is lowered. The field rate is not decreased below the frequency for which excessive flicker will occur. Under the most severe conditions, a frame rate update is employed. This doubles the allocated processing time for all hardware units up to the display processor. As a last resort, the display processor succumbs to a single field mode. Several CT-5 scenes are shown in Figure 4.34. E & S is now selling CT-5 devices at a brisk pace, with some units intended for engineering applications.

4.2.4. McDonnell Douglas Electronics Company

McDonnell Douglas's CIG devices are known as VITAL for virtual image takeoff and landing. VITAL II was the first unit of this type. It was installed on a Pacific Southwest Airline simulator in 1971. VITAL II scenes are constructed entirely from 1200 light points on a black background. A small field of view and sparse scene content combine to limit performance to straight-in landing approaches, with marginal landing capability. The limited scene content does not allow for low-altitude flight or flight outside the runway area. Pilots using this system find it difficult to estimate airspeed and remain oriented in the environment.

VITAL III is a low-cost high-resolution scene generator designed to provide a somewhat richer scene content than the VITAL II. Markings and stripes are displayed on the runway surface. This additional runway detail greatly enhances altitude, airspeed, range, and depth perception during night runway approaches and landings. However, scene content away from the runway is still very sparse.

VITAL III consists of a simple 3-D to 2-D data-base conversion unit which McDonnell Douglas calls the image generation equipment, followed by a unit called a raster blaster, which in turn feeds the display electronics (Figure 4.35). The raster blaster consists of a number of special-purpose computers and controllers, each performing a separate task.

The raster blaster operates upon the polygons resulting from the projections of 3-D objects. A polygon is defined in terms of its left and right edge vector outlines. A polygon is scanned out by moving the electron beam back and forth between its borders (Figure 4.36). Each time the beam reaches a left or right border point, it is displaced vertically to paint out the next scan-line segment. Horizontal beam velocity and vertical separation between segments are carefully controlled to give the displayed surface a uniform appearance.

A conventional CRT writes out scan lines in only one direction. VITAL III's ability to also write right to left allows for a more efficient use of the beam deflection system. The beam position is critical when writing in the retrace mode. The very high beam deflection rate makes the brightness of a scanned surface highly dependent on beam dwell time. Horizontal deflection linearity is critical to picture quality. Variations in the horizontal writing rate result in changes in beam dwell time, creating intensity variations. When the beam is moved from one raster line to the next, any vertical overshoot may cause the beam to overwrite a previously scanned area. Vertical undershoot or variations in line separation also reduce the uniformity of a scanned surface. If partial overwriting occurs along the left and right borders of a scanned polygon, the borders will have an increased brightness and ragged appearance. VITAL III maintains uniformity along the borders by deflecting the beam a small distance past the border, while blanking the beam out during these excursions. The excursion time outside the scanned polygon is used to let the beam circuitry settle down

Figure 4.34. Scenes produced by Evans and Sutherland CT-5 visual system. (Photographs courtesy of Evans and Sutherland and Rediffusion.) (Part c appears in color in the color section.)

(c)

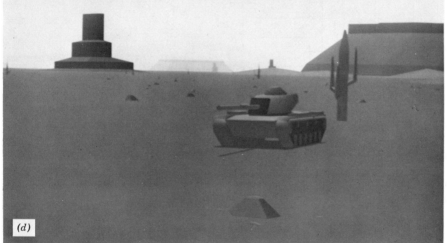

(d)

(e)

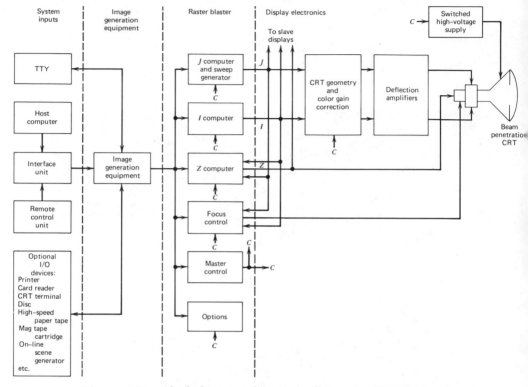

Figure 4.35.   Block diagram of McDonnell Douglas VITAL III unit.

before going on to the next scan line. Relative timing is, of course, critical for this operation.

Image surface generation is handled by I and J computers and a sweep generator. The J computer calculates the left and right border points for each horizontally scanned surface segment. Each time the beam is moved vertically to paint out the next scan-line segment, the J computer adds a ΔJ to the previous J border value. Since the borders of polygons are constructed from vectors, each with a slope of the form $\Delta I/\Delta J$, the computation of ΔJ is a matter of simple mathematics. The J computer also calculates light point data.

The I computer keeps track of the current I value of beam position. It compares the current I position to the I value of the endpoint of the border vector toward which it is scanning. When the endpoint of a border vector is reached, its definition is replaced by that for the next vector in the string. When the scanning of a polygon is complete, the beam blanks out and jumps to the next polygon to be scanned.

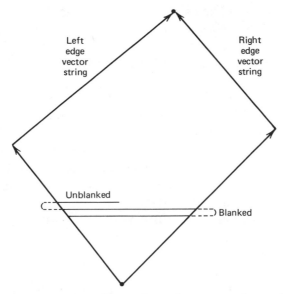

Figure 4.36.   McDonnell Douglas polygon scanning technique.

The sweep generator controls the instantaneous horizontal position of the beam.

A Z computer receives shading coefficients from the image generator. It uses these coefficients to perform a linear interpolation of the intensity values within a surface, as a function of the I and J position. One use of this computer is to provide a tapered horizon glow. The illumination due to landing lights is simulated by tapering the brightness of the runway surface as a function of the distance from the landing aircraft.

A focus controller manages the focus amplifiers of the CRTs. One function is to display a light point at its computed size, regardless of the color of the light. (This is a problem only because of the use of beam-penetration tubes for display.) Beam defocus is needed to eliminate the visibility of individual lines when filled polygonal surfaces are scanned out. Defocus is used very carefully to prevent edges from losing their sharpness. Special care is taken when scanning out small polygons to keep the beam focused well enough to prevent a fuzzy appearance. For large surfaces, the combination of a lower line density and defocused beam increases scanning efficiency.

Current McDonnell Douglas units are known as VITAL IV. The VITAL IV data base consists of light strings and surfaces. Each light string requires 13 data words and each surface 19 words. Any combination of light strings and surfaces can be used as long as the data-base capacity of 9100 memory locations is not exceeded. Typically, a data base includes a fully marked CAT III runway, which requires 215 light strings. The remaining data-base capacity is distributed over enroute, approach, and airport areas.

The VITAL IV image generation equipment for a single channel is stored in a single cabinet. The cabinet contains a Sperry Univac (formerly Varian) V-76 computer with 64K words of semiconductor memory, special-purpose computation hardware, and power supplies (Figure 4.37). The output of the general-purpose computer passes to a transformation arithmetic scene converter (TASC) via a priority memory access controller (PMAC). TASC performs translation, rotation, and intensity computations in pipeline fashion. The results are sent to a raster blaster–occulter–shader section, which transforms 2-D scene data into display drive signals.

VITAL IV display electronics consist of deflection amplifiers, a high-voltage switching power supply, focus and video amplifiers, and geometric and gain correction circuitry. Beam penetration CRTs (21 or 25 inches), with a red-green phosphor mix, are used. The red phosphor is activated by the lower voltage (6 kV) while the green responds to the higher voltage (12 kV). Intermediate voltages produce orange to yellow colors.

The colors are displayed sequentially, each display frame in the order red/orange/yellow/green/yellow orange. The display is refreshed at a rate of 30 times per second. Light points are drawn by blanking the beam, deflecting it to the proper screen position, allowing the beam circuitry to settle down, and finally unblanking the beam to draw the light point. The beam settling time is dependent upon the deflection distance from the previous light point. Light point display time varies from 3.5 to 22.5 microseconds, depending upon light point spacing. Surfaces are displayed by alternately blanking, then unblanking the beam while painting a raster structure within the surface boundary. The raster direction may be either vertical or horizontal; the raster density selectable from 256 to 1024. Occulting is accomplished through the use of vertical separation planes. Any color may be used for occulting, but all occulting surfaces must be the same color.

The VITAL IV display unit contains a spherical mirror and beam splitter to provide the pilot with collimated imagery. The field of view provided by the standard display is 35° vertical by 45° horizontal. McDonnell Douglas is also developing helmet mounted displays utilizing Honeywell optics (Figure 4.38). A VITAL IV scene is shown in Figure 4.39.

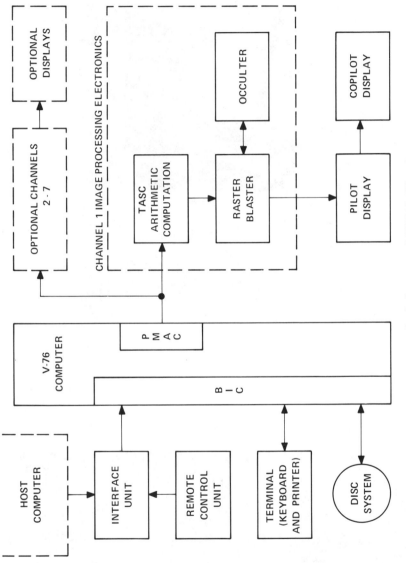

Figure 4.37. Block diagram of VITAL IV unit.

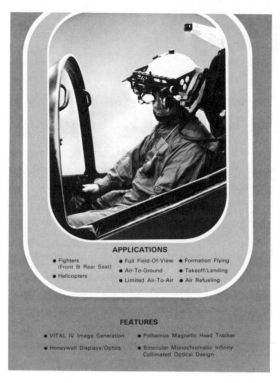

Figure 4.38. VITAL helmet mounted visual, preliminary fact sheet.

Figure 4.39. Scene produced by VITAL IV visual system.

4.2.5. Gould GVS-1 System

Gould is developing a medium-performance image generator capable of a 30 frame per second update rate (Figure 4.40) [DICH80, DICH81].* At the front end of the system is a general-purpose computer, which performs the usual tasks of data-base retrieval, data management, bookkeeping, communication with the aircraft simulator, and control of the other image generation subsystems. The second stage is a high-speed geometric processor built from a distributed network of LSI elements. It performs 3-D transforms, elimination of back-facing faces, clipping, and priority processing.

A display generator takes digital inputs from the general-purpose computer and geometric processor and converts them to full-color analog video. It is centered around a double buffer ping-pong memory to and from which simultaneous read and write operations are performed. As the data from the geometric processor are being stored into one buffer, the past frame's data are being read out of the other buffer. Each buffer consists of 54 memory planes. Each memory plane holds a screen-size bit map of image information (but not the image itself). The storage operation into the ping buffer is performed with random access, while the pong buffer is read in raster format. At the completion of a frame read the roles of the buffers switch.

The buffer storage operation is divided into a number of subtasks: face-edge outline generation, face-edge priority storage, and computation of edge smoothing coefficients. Face-edge outline generation is performed by a vector generator using a data list received from the geometric processor. This list contains face-edge endpoints expressed to subpixel precision. The vector generator extends an edge one full pixel at a time between each pair of face-edge endpoints. Before data are stored into a pixel location, they are compared with the existing edge and smoothing data to determine (1) whether the edge is the highest priority edge passing through the pixel, and (2) whether other edges of the same object already pass through the pixel. After these determinations are made, new smoothing data are stored in their proper priority relationship in memory planes dedicated to smoothing data. Smoothing coefficients are determined by table lookup, based entirely on subpixel entry and exit coordinates and edge polarity. The uppermost and lowermost vertices of a face are treated as a special case. For these, edge data are not stored, but smoothing data still are.

During the read cycle, the refresh memory is addressed in raster order.

---

*Gould has suspended development of the system.

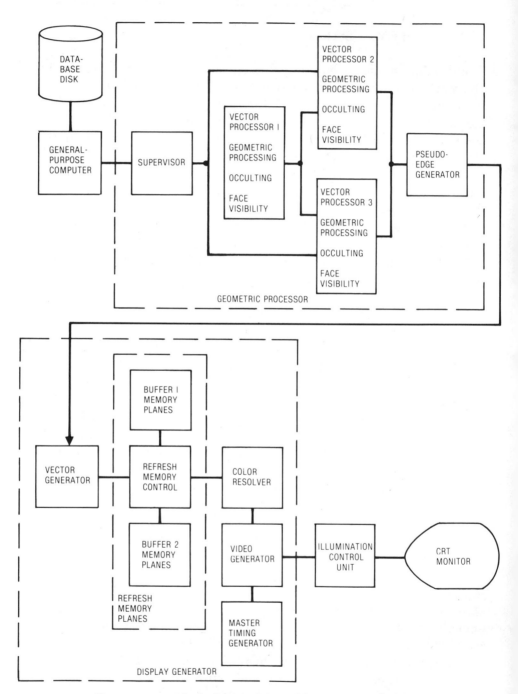

Figure 4.40. Block diagram of Gould GVS-1 visual system.

During this cycle, face outlines are filled in, hidden surfaces are eliminated, and edges are smoothed. Faces are filled in by traversing the area bounded by the face-edge outline, one scan line at a time. This procedure is not used for the uppermost and lowermost vertices of a face, since both left and right borders fall within a single pixel. Since these portions of the face do not exist in the memory planes dedicated to face color filling, the information must be recovered from the planes dedicated to edge smoothing data. For pixels interior to a face, the stored face data serve as an index to a lookup table. For pixels crossed by edges (except for the uppermost and lowermost vertices), additional logical tests take place using the stored color, priority, and edge information. For this condition, simultaneous table lookups are performed, with the retrieved data mixed according to the computed smoothing factors. The outputs in either case are digital color codes representing red, green, and blue color components which are converted to analog video by D/A converters.

An illumination control unit combines the analog inputs received from the display generator with control parameters obtained from the general-purpose computer to add the atmospheric and illumination effects of horizon glow, haze, and curved-surface shading. The output of each illumination control unit feeds a CRT (Figure 4.41).

4.2.6. Advanced Technology Systems (ATS)

ATS is a New Jersey based division of the privately owned Austin Company. Their first CIG device was a night-only visual system designed for navigating a ship through a harbor. It displays 300 light points (colored, hooded, and blinking).

ATS will provide a visual system for the U.S. Navy's new Weapons Tactics Trainer (WTT) [SHOH79, SINO80]. The WTT is a simulator system being built by the Hughes Aircraft Company for training pilots to fly the F-18 aircraft. It is a two-cockpit system which will be used primarily to train pilots for dogfighting and for ground attack maneuvers such as subsonic missions launched from aircraft carriers. The Navy is scheduled to begin training with the device in October 1982.

ATS claims to have a flexible design emphasizing speed and processing capacity (Figure 4.42). It claims that the system, called COMPUTROL®, will process 40,000 edges and 10,000 light points (over all channels) at a 30 frame per second update rate. A large number of special effects are planned, including translucency, curved-surface shading, fog, clouds, tapered horizon glow, and an unlimited number of moving objects.

Figure 4.41.   A scene produced by the Gould GVS-1 system before work was suspended on it. The display generator developed the scene in real time. However, the scene is static in that the display list was stored in PROM.

COMPUTROL is based upon ECL MSI logic. Unlike the other visual systems discussed in this chapter, it does not require a general-purpose computer as its host. A custom-built CPU manages the image generation process. The CPU controls arithmetic operations, initiates data transfers, and manages other special-purpose control units distributed throughout the system. The CPU is able to handle 25×10^6 instructions per second via pipeline decoding of instructions from an internal demand instruction cache. The CPU makes use of other floating-point units residing in the system when they are not performing their primary assigned tasks.

At the heart of the image generation hardware lie two parallel processors, a projection processor and a visible surface processor. Each processor consists of very-high-speed controllers and arithmetic units which communicate with the CPU and main memory.

The projection processor retrieves data from disk, projects the 3-D environment description onto a 2-D view plane for each channel, clips edges passing between up to 512 pyramids of view for a 360° × 360° image, and reformats, sorts, and stores the resulting potentially visible edge and light

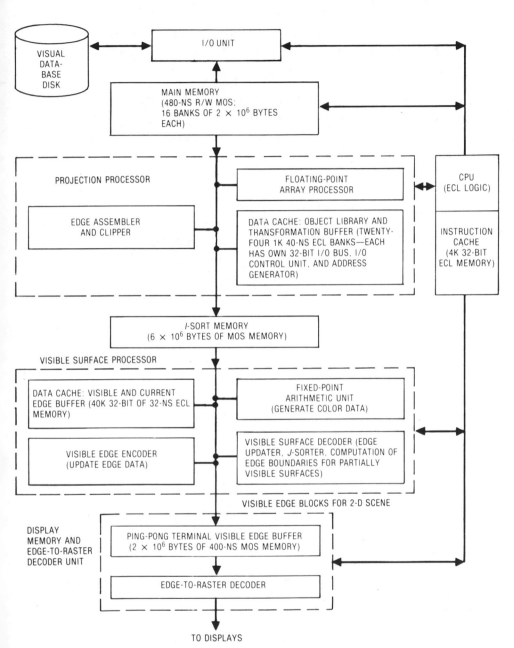

Figure 4.42. Block diagram of ATS COMPUTROL.

point data. The projection processor consists of a floating-point array processor, an edge assembler and clipper, a data cache, and other logic and fixed-point arithmetic units.

The floating-point array processor is loaded by the CPU with data and/ or pointers to data in cache. Perspective projection is a shared task of the CPU and the array processor. The projection of an edge requires a total of 30 multiplies and 30 adds, performed in parallel by two multipliers and two adders. The computation time is 40 nanoseconds $\times$ 30/2 = 60 nanoseconds per edge.

The edge assembler and clipper first performs clipping by using four comparators to test the left and right and/or top and bottom of an edge to determine whether it lies within a view window. If an edge is clipped, approximately nine floating-point adds and nine floating-point multiplies are required to derive new endpoints for the edge. The final tasks are to transform edges into the form required by the visible surface generator, to construct a system of pointers which will later be used in the ordering of edges by scan-line number, and to place the resulting data into an I-sort memory. Data specifying an edge include its starting and stopping endpoints, slope, and shading values.

The I-sort memory has a ping-pong structure, with each side of the memory operating independently. During one frame's time, as data are being written to the ping side of the memory by the projection processor, the previous frame's data are being read from the pong side of the memory by the visible surface processor. The I-sort memory consists of 6×10^6 bytes MOS, in which data pertaining to the generated edges are stored and sorted with respect to initial I values (i.e., the number of the scan line at which the uppermost vertex of the clipped edge resides). Approximately 400 bits are required to store the data for an edge once they are sorted by I values.

The visible surface processor takes I-sorted, potentially visible edges and, for each scan line, calculates the J intercepts of the edges. Then it sorts the edge intercepts along a scan line and solves the hidden-surface problem on a scan-line-segment by scan-line-segment basis. These operations are performed by a number of subunits: the fixed-point arithmetic processor, the data cache (visible and current edge buffer), the visible surface decoder and edge sorter, the visible edge encoder, and internal hardwired control logic.

The visible surface decoder and edge sorter scan the previous scan line's edge list and add new edges (i.e., those that start on the scan line currently being processed). As each edge is encountered, its J intercept along the scan line is computed to 21-bit accuracy, and then sent to a J

Plate 1

Plate 2
Plate 3

Plate 1. Night scene produced by a GE third-generation visual simulator.

Plate 2. A photograph taken from Singer/Link's visual system delivered to All Nipon Airways.

Plate 3. Scene produced by an Evans and Sutherland image generator.

Plate 4. Scene produced by a nonreal-time setup at Grumman.

Plate 5. Scene produced by Evans and Sutherland CT-5 visual system. (Photograph courtesy of Evans and Sutherland and Redifon.)

Plate 4

Plate 5

Plate 6. Scene produced by the GE B-52 visual simulator. Note the excellent texture on the surfaces.

Plate 7. Scene taken from GE COFT instructor's console. The recticle and range marks are shown in the foreground as they would be seen through the trainee's viewing scope.

bucket sort unit which uses 9 of the 18 most significant bits for sorting, placing the remaining 9 and a pointer back to the rest of the edge data into cache. The J-sort unit then performs a second pass on the data using the remaining 9 bits. Next the sorted edge data are again scanned to compute the distance between the viewpoint and each surface segment on a scan line. The closest segments are marked "visible."

The visible edge encoder works in parallel with the visible surface decoder to determine and interpolate color data.

The final stage of processing is handled by a display memory and edge-to-raster decoder units. These units receive visible edge blocks for the 2-D scene. They buffer and convert these data into smooth shaded analog video.

The WTT enclosure consists of two domes, each 40 feet in diameter and each surrounding a mock F-18 cockpit. The two domes will be used interactively for air-to-air combat practice. The inside surfaces of the domes are large spherical screens. Each dome will contain five projectors [MILI80], each receiving video signals from a different image generation channel. Three GE light valves will project a hemispheric sky–earth scene. Two specially designed Hughes projectors will provide missile, target, and gunfire imagery.

4.2.7. Marconi Radar Systems Ltd.

Marconi Radar began developing an image generation capability in 1971. Their first systems were delivered in 1977. They are weapon aimers and optical trackers having a narrow field of view of from 2° to 28°. Scene content is limited to foreground groups of targets against a simple backdrop. The next product developed was a device for training the bridge team of large ships.

Marconi is nearing production of a unit with complete visual capability for flight simulation. They claim that the generated imagery will contain highly realistic static and dynamic textures at three levels of detail [ROWL80]. Marconi is now working jointly with Sperry Rand in the United States.

4.2.8. Other Approaches

The view ray approach to displaying a grid data base in perspective was developed by Bob Heartz of GE in 1973 and is described by Bunker and

Figure 4.43.   A scene produced by a non-real-time setup at Grumman. (This photograph is reproduced in color in the color section.)

Heartz [BUNK75]. A team headed by Heartz has built a device that can generate a scene in about 30 seconds.

Boeing [ELSO81] is in the second phase of a three-phase CIG project funded by the Defense Advanced Research Projects Agency (DARPA). The long-range goal is the development of a family of image generation devices most likely employing VLSI technology. Boeing expects to have a non-real-time brassboard in operation by 1984. Instead of storing objects by their edge outlines, Boeing plans to store rules for generating the objects. It claims that this approach will result in an order of magnitude increase in scene detail over current systems.

Grumman [GARD78, GARD79a, GARD79b] is pursuing a unique no-edge approach to CIG based upon functional models. A scene is modeled as a set of convex objects, with each object defined by one quadric surface and up to six bounding planes. A 25-parameter Fourier-based texture model is used to add detail to scene surfaces. An image produced by this approach, created in non-real-time, is shown in Figure 4.43. Grumman expects to build a real-time operational prototype by 1985. Its unique algorithms for surface visibility, shading, and texturing will be implemented with a highly modular, parallel system architecture.

Honeywell [SOLA81] has completed two phases of a program to determine the hardware requirements for the real-time display of curved terrain surfaces. Its approach treats the landscape as a patchwork of bicubic splines, each defined by the equation

$$\text{elevation} = a_0 + a_1 x + a_2 y + a_3 x^2 + a_4 y^2 + a_5 xy + \cdots + a_{15} x^3 y^3$$

The projection of a patch boundary onto the view window is a curved line (Figure 4.44). Thus unlike for triangular terrain surfaces, the projections of the corners of a bicubic patch cannot simply be joined by straight lines on the view window. In fact, to display a bicubic landscape requires a sizable computational and memory capability and complex solutions to such common operations as antialiasing and shadowing.

Honeywell's real-time display approach combines two concepts. First, a z buffer is used to assemble the view plane components of a scene [CATM74]. Second, a quad-tree data structure is used to organize the terrain patches (Figure 4.45). The root node of the tree represents a square mission area. Each of its four daughter nodes represents quadrants of the parent area, and so on down the tree. A picture is generated by scanning the data in as many nodes as is necessary to determine the scene to the

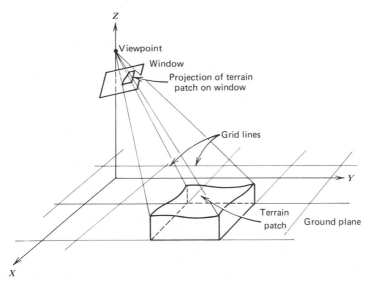

Figure 4.44. Illustration of Honeywell's terrain representation approach. (From [SOLA81].)

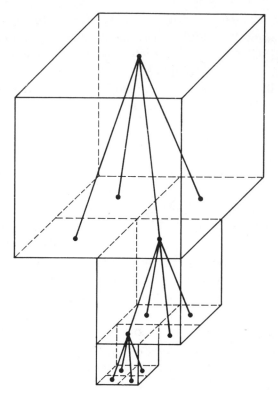

Figure 4.45.   Illustration of quad-tree data structure.

required detail. Each node in the tree carries a flag to indicate whether it is a terminal or a nonterminal node, the X and Y coordinates of a specified corner of the associated patch, and the length of the sides of the patch. Nonterminal nodes also carry the elevation at each of the four corners of the patch, the intensity (average intensity of the four subnodes), and pointers to the four subnodes. Terminal nodes carry a 16-entry array, which is a bicubic representation of the patch, and a 2^k by 2^k texture map for the patch.

Honeywell's tree traversal starts with the top node. The picture area corresponding to that node is determined by projecting its four corner points to the view plane. A decision is then made whether to terminate the traversal at that node or proceed to the next level down the tree. Termination of the traversal down a branch occurs when one of the following three conditions is fulfilled. (1) The projected area represented by the node falls outside the view window. (2) The projected area is small enough to display. (3) The projected area faces away from the observer.

When the entire tree has been traversed in this manner, the result is the identification of all potentially visible nodes. The resolution of priority conflicts among these nodes is handled by a z buffer, which is a combination of a frame buffer and a distance buffer. The frame buffer holds the intensities of display points as they are generated. The distance buffer stores the ranges of these points. Priority conflicts are solved by keeping only the nearest such points when conflicts occur. Since the distance to each displayed point is known, the simulation of atmospheric attenuation is simple.

Aviation Simulation Technology manufactures a very-low-cost scene generator based upon dual Intel 8085 microprocessors. The scenes produced consist of a ground plane, horizon, and runway, with lights along the runway (Figure 4.46). The imagery is raster scan and is updated 30 times per second.

A number of other companies, including Le Matériel Téléphonique [GILL80], Hitachi, Technology Service Company, Hughes Aircraft, Krupp, and Saab, are investigating real-time graphics, or are at least rumored to be

Figure 4.46. Aviation Simulation Technology twin engine flight simulator showing visual display in upper left.

doing so. A number of theses have been written on the subject [ANDE77, PAPA77, RAMJ79, WEIN82].

4.3. DISPLAY APPROACHES

4.3.1. Image Source Devices

Most image source devices [GUM79] fall into one of two categories, CRTs or projectors. A CRT image is always viewed by the pilot through an optical system. The optical system collimates the image and increases the field of view. Projection devices (which often themselves use CRT technology) project images onto screens, which are either viewed directly or through optical systems.

Monochromatic CRTs as large as 36 inches have been built for use in simulators (Figure 4.47). Multicolor calligraphic CIG systems often use beam-penetration tubes in which a single electron gun paints out line segments and points. A limited set of colors is obtained by varying the degree of beam penetration. The continuous nature of the phosphor surface allows the tubes to be used at high resolution.

Devices producing images in raster format often use shadow-mask CRTs. Shadow-mask tubes are based upon triads of phosphors (red, green, and blue). Three electron guns are directed toward an aperture mask which allows each beam to strike only the correct set of phosphor dots. Shadow-mask tubes offer a higher brightness and wider range of colors than beam-penetration tubes; their disadvantages include quantization effects and color registration problems.

A hybrid approach is also possible. The Evans and Sutherland SP2 device uses a specially designed calligraphically driven shadow-mask CRT—with very good results.

Projection systems in use today are primarily television based [HEND75]. Some project simple monochrome or color CRT images through optical systems. Others combine separate red, green, and blue image components to form a single full-color picture.

Another class of projectors modulate video signals with light valves to form projected images. Their operation is extremely complex and is only touched upon here. The most popular light valve is the GE full-color single-beam device (Figure 4.48), which uses a video signal to velocity-modulate an electron beam [GOOD75]. The beam writes diffraction gratings onto an oil film, which is imaged through a Schlieren optical system.

Figure 4.47.   A 36-inch CRT built by Thomas Electronics.

Concentrating the electron beam onto any pixel area of the oil film deforms the area into an elemental lens.

The GE light valve is fed from behind by an external white light source. A color plate and lenticular lens are in front of the light source. An input slot assembly lies in front of the lenticular lens. White light traveling through the green portion of the color filter plate passes through the horizontal input slots. Green light reaching the oil film is modulated by raster lines written onto the oil film by the electron beam. The raster line width is controlled by means of a high-frequency carrier which is applied to vertical beam deflection plates. This carrier is, in turn, modulated by the green video signal. The green light emerging from the oil film is diffracted off output bars located inside a Schlieren projection assembly.

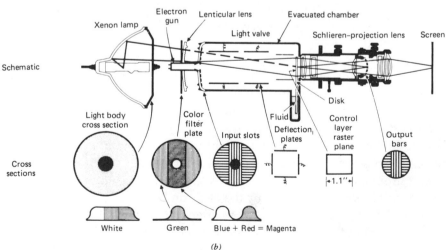

Figure 4.48. GE light valve: (a) Photograph. (b) Schematics. (From [GOOD75].)

| Model | Light Output in Lumens | | | Resolution in TV Lines per Picture Height | | Scan Standard |
	Open Gate Minimum	Modulated TV Minimum	Modulated TV Typical	Minimum Horizontal	Minimum Vertical	
GE color projectors						
PJ 5100	550	200	280	750	650	1023 lines
PJ 5150	1250	500	650	750	650	1023 lines
GE monochrome projectors						
PJ 7150	1700	1000	1250	800	750	1023 lines
PJ 7155	3300	2000	2400	800	750	1023 lines

Figure 4.48. (c) Specifications for several models.

White light also passes through the magenta (red plus blue) portion of the color filter plate. The resulting magenta light travels through vertical input slots. The magenta light is modulated by vertical diffraction gratings written onto the oil film surface. These vertical diffraction gratings are formed by velocity-modulating the electron beam spot in the horizontal direction. For the red part of the spectrum, a 16-MHz carrier signal is applied to the horizontal beam deflection plates. The 16-MHz carrier is modulated by the red video signal. The grooves thus written onto the oil film surface have the proper spacing to diffract the red portion of the spectrum, while blocking the blue.

For blue, a 12-MHz carrier signal is applied to the horizontal beam deflection plates. This carrier is modulated by the blue video signal. The grooves written onto the oil film by the 12-MHz carrier diffract the blue portion of the spectrum through the output slots, while blocking the red.

The GE light valve yields a moderately bright image (see Figure 4.48c), has high resolution, and has a relatively low cost. Since a single electron gun is used, there is no problem of registering the three color components of the image. One limitation, however, is the fixed nature of the design.

The Hughes liquid-crystal light valve consists of a sandwich of thin films which electrically control the birefringence of a thin-film liquid-crystal layer [GOOD75, BLEH78]. The general configuration of the device is shown in Figure 4.49. A low-voltage audio-frequency power supply is connected to the two outer thin-film indium-tin-oxide transparent electrodes and thus across the entire thin-film sandwich. A cadmium sulfide photoconductor and cadmium telluride light-blocking layer combine to create a rectifying heterojunction. A dielectric mirror and the blocking layer separate the photoconductor from the readout light beam.

A CRT image is coupled to the Hughes light valve through either fiber optics or relay lenses. The photoconductor acts as an imaging light-controlled voltage-modulator for the liquid-crystal layer. In operation, with the ac voltage bias across the sandwich structure and no imaging light incident on the photoconductor, most of the bias falls across the photoconductor. Then, in response to the input light pattern, the photoconductor impedance lowers and the bias voltage is switched to the liquid-crystal layer. This drives the layer above its electrooptical threshold in a pattern that replicates the input image intensity in the form of a birefringent pattern. The cell is illuminated from behind by collimated light. The light travels through the liquid-crystal layer to the dielectric mirror. The mirror reflects the light back through the liquid-crystal layer and out the cell. The birefringent pattern on the liquid-crystal layer causes a rotation of the axis of polarization, which permits the projected light to

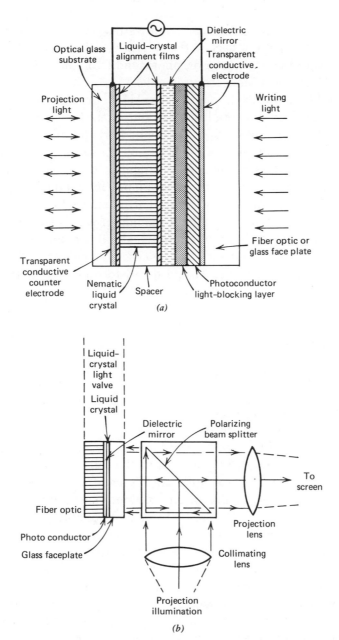

Figure 4.49. Hughes liquid crystal light valve. (From [BLEH78].) (*a*) Cross-sectional schematic of light valve. (*b*) Light valve projection system.

pass through a polarizing filter (prism) toward a screen. The prism returns the liquid-crystal pattern back to the correct visible image. The illumination lamp, liquid-crystal material, photoconductor, and CRT can be chosen to meet specific system requirements.

A titus-tube light valve is manufactured by Sodern Company of France. The titus tube is an electron-beam Pockels-effect imaging device which uses a KD_2PO_4 plate operated just below its Curie temperature in a reflection mode. The titus light valve operates on the basis of the variation in birefringence in a crystal when an electrical field is applied through the crystal in the direction of light propagation. The operation is similar to that of the liquid-crystal light valve in that an external projection lamp, a polarizer/analyzer prism, and a light modulator are used. The titus light valve is capable of high luminous output, exhibits no noticeable scan-line structure or flicker, possesses random-access image-writing capability, and can be designed to compensate for distortions; but it is slow and extremely expensive.

4.3.2. Optical Systems

This discussion follows the excellent tutorial given by LaRussa [LARU79].

Optical systems can be pupil forming or non-pupil forming. With a pupil-forming system, an observer must keep his head within a specific viewing volume. With a non-pupil-forming system, the observer can move his head off the display axis until the falloff in illumination becomes objectionable. The basic difference is a matter of degree. The falloff in illumination is sharp with a pupil-forming system, but gradual with a non-pupil-forming system. There are three types of optical systems which we will discuss: screens, refractors, and reflectors.

Both front-projection and rear-projection diffusing screens (Figure 4.50) can be designed which do not form a pupil. They can be transformed into quasi-pupil-forming systems by increasing the gain of the screen so that the projected image is directed toward a particular viewing volume (dashed lines in the diagrams). In non- and quasi-pupil-forming systems the projected image appears to be at the distance of the screen from the observer.

Refractive infinity optical systems are more compact than systems that use screens, but require more optical elements and are more complex and costly. Refractive systems can be designed which are either pupil forming or non-pupil forming.

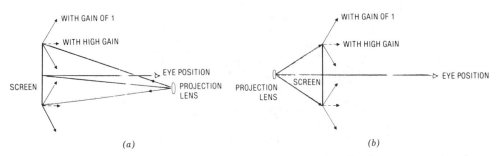

Figure 4.50. Projection screens (apparent brightness = brightness × gain of screen). (a) Front projection screen. (b) Rear projection screen.

Reflective systems (Figure 4.51) are very popular today. They offer a wider field of view than lenses, with less color distortion. Reflective systems use a collimating eyepiece mirror as their final element. If the eyepiece mirror is fed by an optical projection element (such as a spherical mirror), a true pupil is formed. If the eyepiece mirror is fed by a diffusing screen (such as a CRT), no pupil is formed. One popular reflective system is Farrand Optical Company's compact unit, called a Pancake Window™. This device produces a very wide circular field of view (on the order of 90°) and does so with a maximum eye relief. The unit consists of an eyepiece mirror and beam-splitter package. The unit is an in-line display, that is, the mirror, beam splitter, and image source are all normal to the line of sight (Figure 4.52). Pancake Windows are often used in conjunction with light valves which produce a polarized image output. By align-

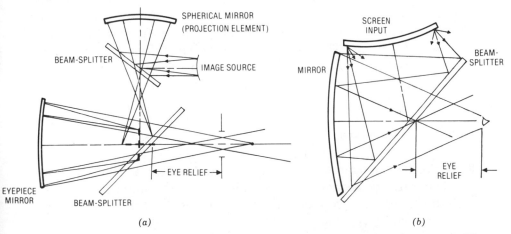

Figure 4.51. Reflective systems. (From [LARU79].) (a) Pupil-forming system. (b) Non-pupil-forming system.

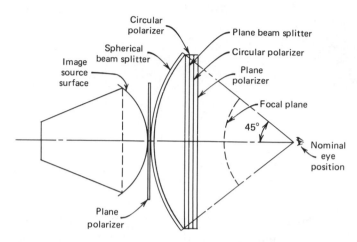

Figure 4.52.   Farrand Optical Company's Pancake Window™.

ing the axis of polarization of the image with that of the window, the throughput of the window is effectively doubled. Recently the width of the Pancake Window has been reduced from 12 inches to ⅝ inch through the use of a holographic analog of the spherical eyepiece mirror [LARU78]. This new device is still experimental.

Farrand also offers a helmet mounted Pancake Window display system with a total instantaneous field of view of 135° horizontal by 60° vertical. Each eye is furnished with an 80° horizontal by 60° vertical field of view, the overlap between eyes is 25°. Imagery is carried to the display by two fiberoptic cables, one for each eye. The system forms an aerial image just in front of a beam splitter, which when viewed through the Pancake Window eyepiece provides pilots with an infinity display with a 15-mm diameter at their eyes. This infinity display will have a brightness of about 1 percent the brightness of the fiberoptic input. The pilot looks through the beam splitter to see the interior of the cockpit and its instruments.

4.3.3.   Configurations

Three display configurations in wide use are (1) dome screen with internal light valve projection, (2) dodecahedron with external light valve projection and infinity optics, and (3) helmet mounted display. Each has certain drawbacks.

Dome systems are large (20 to 40 feet in diameter) and expensive. They are used mainly for practicing aerial combat and aircraft carrier landings.

They have one or more projectors for the background imagery and one or more for the foreground objects. The complexity of coordinating a number of separate projectors is a major problem. Since the background scene covers a wider area than the foreground objects, the background brightness is very low (on the order of 1 foot-lambert). Both sets of projectors may be slaved to the pilot's head or eye motion so that only a minimal instantaneous field of view need be generated. This also adds to the complexity of the system.

A dodecahedron infinity display system requires a smaller volume than a dome, but is very heavy and rather unwieldy. A separate projector is required for every live face of the dodecahedron. The imagery will have a brightness of over 6 foot-lamberts over the entire display. This approach is often used for monochrome systems.

A helmet mounted display can achieve a high resolution over the entire sphere of vision, since the CIG need only generate an area of interest scene for the direction in which the pilot's head is pointed. Advantages are small size and low cost. The main disadvantages are the unnaturalness of wearing a display on one's head and the need to use a beam splitter to allow the pilot to view the aircraft instrumentation.

4.4. VISUAL FLIGHT SIMULATION IN THE 1980s

Some persons in the industry believe that the future of image generation hardware lies with VLSI circuitry; such a view is expressed by Cohen and Demetrescu [COHE80]. The idea is to employ an architecture built around a large number of identical VLSI processors. The aim is to combine simplicity in design with the speed of parallelism. Others believe that a more traditional architecture using gate arrays will prove cheaper and more practical.

All supporting software for visual flight simulation will have to be written using a top-down structured design approach. Companies not using modern software engineering practices will find that decreasing hardware costs are more than offset by rising software costs. The data-base development process will have to be automated using Defense Mapping Agency terrain and culture files for input; interactive computer graphic techniques are alone too expensive for developing large hierarchical data bases and will prove feasible only for small areas of special interest. If the government develops a suitable data-base standard in the 1980s, then data bases developed by any one company could be used to drive simulators built by all other companies. This would reduce the duplication of effort

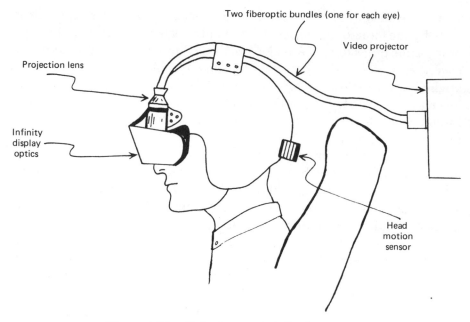

Figure 4.53.   Helmet mounted display system.

now taking place in data-base design. The optical disk may eventually replace the magnetic disk as a data-base storage medium. Read/write optical disks are being worked on by a number of companies and may emerge in the mid to late 1980s.

Holographic approaches are attracting interest for image display. Some future systems may use trichromatic holographic Pancake Windows in conjunction with new designs of light valves. A second approach mounts a Pancake Window assembly on the pilot's helmet (Figure 4.53). The pilot's head direction is continuously tracked to obtain data needed to generate a high-detail area-of-interest scene. A miniature fiberoptic/lens system mounted on the helmet projects the area-of-interest image to the pilot's eyes [WOOD79]. The pilot looks through the beam splitter to see a lower detailed background scene and the aircraft instrumentation. Other future systems may employ laser projectors [YAMA75].

5 DIGITAL IMAGE ANOMALIES: STATIC AND DYNAMIC

NICHOLAS S. SZABO

5.1. INTRODUCTION

When CIG systems were first developed, a number of image anomalies became apparent. These anomalies were somewhat puzzling at first because similar problems were not encountered in conventional television. Although the underlying mathematical reasons for these problems were well understood from known theories [PEAR75], the interrelation of the physical phenomena with human perception was not well known. This chapter explains these image anomalies in terms of human perception.

Fundamentally, all the anomalies are due to the fact that computer-generated images are created by sampling processes, in both the space and the time domains. Since the data base consists of polyhedra with infinitely sharp edges, the scene prior to the sampling process is not spatial frequency limited. This implies, according to the Nyquist criterion, that aliasing will occur. Such aliasing effects are often called scintillation or rastering.

Although, in the general case, only a very small percent of the picture elements scintillate, the effect is rather disturbing. This is because the human visual system is instinctively change sensitive; for example, a flashing light or moving object is much more noticeable than a steady one. Aliasing unfortunately typically manifests itself as a recurring change, either in intensity or in apparent position or shape. Such distracting effects are particularly counterproductive in flight training because the objective of the training is to teach the student to react to subtle visual cues.

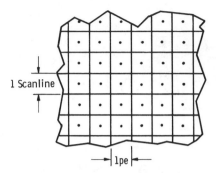

Figure 5.1. Image mosaic.

To understand aliasing, one must understand the digital image generation process. The display consists of a mosaic of picture elements, as shown in Figure 5.1. The intensity and color of each picture element are computed for the infinitesimal point at the center of the picture element (pixel). This computation is performed once per field or frame time. Since in typical applications, the area subtended by the picture element is larger than the resolving power of the eye, each picture element is discernible. Consequently these anomalies are not masked by the limited resolution of the eye.

5.2.   CONVENTIONAL VERSUS SAMPLED IMAGES

There are some important differences between digitally generated images and those produced by conventional television. The horizontal scan in conventional television is a continuous analog process, while in the vertical direction the image is sampled 525 times. One way the sampling process in conventional television differs from that of CGI is that the sampling shape is not infinitesimal but has a Gaussian distribution. This means that instead of taking into account only what occurs at the geometric center of a picture element, the Gaussian-weighted average intensity of each pixel is determined. This process of averaging in the spatial domain is equivalent to a low-pass filter process in the spatial frequency domain. As a result, in TV the input information is band-limited.

Digitally generated images are also sampled in the time domain, at either the field or the frame rate. This sampling process again differs from time domain sampling in a vidicon tube. For CIG the sampling pulse is infinitely short, while for the vidicon tube the output results from the input light integrated over the field interval.

Because for CIG both the field and the frame time intervals are significantly shorter than the time response of the eye (for moderate light

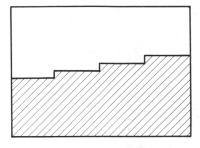

Figure 5.2. Stairstepping as might be seen on a nearly horizontal edge.

conditions), one might expect that aliasing due to undersampling in the time domain would not be noticeable. However, as will be shown, this is not true. As the eye tracks a moving object, the human mind translates an otherwise imperceptible time delay into a displacement, in a manner very similar to a stroboscope that stops motion.

It is important to distinguish between temporal and spatial aliasing because the suppression of each requires different techniques.

5.3. SPATIAL ALIASING

The most frequently noticed problem of a digitally generated image is *stairstepping*. This effect occurs at the border of two contrasting surfaces when the edge separating them is nearly parallel or perpendicular to the scan line (Figure 5.2). While stairstepping is noticeable even on a static image, the human mind has a tendency to disregard it. In dynamic situations this problem is much more noticeable. As shown in Figure 5.3, the rolling of the aircraft will result in the steps becoming shorter as the angle with the horizon increases. The human is attracted to this apparent rippling of the nearly horizontal line.

Aliasing is also noticeable when the width of a stripe is on the order of that of a picture element. The stripe may either hit or miss the center of picture elements (Figure 5.4). This will result in *line breakup*, which is

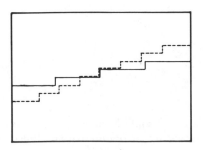

Figure 5.3.   Nearly horizontal edge as seen on successive frames from an aircraft in roll.

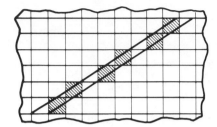

Figure 5.4.   Illustration of line breakup.

further aggravated by the movement of the scene. With movement, a gap in the line will appear to shift back and forth in a puzzling fashion.

Crawling is another phenomenon that is disturbing to the eye because it suggests that the shape of an object is changing. Figure 5.5 illustrates this phenomenon. Even very slight changes in position or attitude may result in sudden variations in size when an edge passes through the center of a picture element.

Yet another anomaly may occur when a very small face moves across the screen. The small face may either miss or pass over the center of a picture element. In the former case the face will not be displayed, whereas in the latter instance it will be displayed as an entire pixel (Figure 5.6). The resulting phenomenon is called *scintillation* and can be highly distracting.

Using sample data theory techniques, one could theoretically eliminate all aliasing by frequency limiting the input image in the spatial domain to one-half of the sampling frequency. Such filtering in the spatial domain corresponds to convolving the image with a (sin x)/x function. The resultant image would then be sampled.

Unfortunately this convolution process is not realizable with a reasonable amount of hardware. However, it may be approximated by intensity averaging by area. It has been found that merely computing the average (according to area) intensity of each picture element yields a greatly improved image. This is illustrated in Figures 5.7 and 5.8. This algorithm

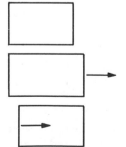

Figure 5.5.   Crawling of a horizontally moving object. A rectangle as it may appear at three different display times.

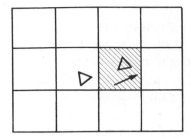

Figure 5.6. Scintillation caused by a small face translated through the image mosaic.

will of course result in an inaccurate representation of a scene, because the pixels bisected by an edge will have an intensity different from that in the real world. However, experiments have shown that even though the individual pixels are resolvable by the eye, the observer will not interpret these transitional picture elements as separate faces of unique intensities. The observer interprets the assigned intensities I_2 and I_3 shown in Figure 5.8 to mean a displacement of an edge.

The intensity-averaging-by-area method explained here is in fact a rather crude approximation of convolution by (sin x)/x in the spatial domain, since it corresponds to convolution with a box function (Figure 5.9). It is certainly possible to approximate (sin x)/x more closely, such as shown by the two pyramid functions in Figures 5.10 and 5.11. Better approximations are more costly in terms of hardware.

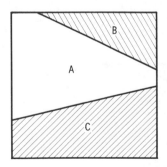

Figure 5.7.   Intensity averaging by area. The intensity of the entire picture element (or pixel) is computed as a weighted average of the intensities of subpixel regions A, B, and C.

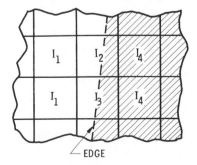

Figure 5.8.   Transition between light and dark areas. Intensities I_2 and I_3 are computed by the intensity averaging method. These pixels are not interpreted as separate faces by the eye.

Over the years a number of methods for implementing the spatial filtering process have been tried. One method divides each scan line into subscan lines, and each pixel into subpixels. In effect, each displayed pixel's intensity is a function of the intensities of its subpixels (e.g., the mean intensity of the subpixel centers). The exact methods used for this computation and the shapes of the spatial filters are closely held secrets of the CIG companies.

While the exact shape of the spatial filter is probably not too important, it appears that the basic requirement is correctly expressed by a statement attributed to Erdahl (see [SCHU80]):

> *The total energy contributed to all display pixels by a scene fragment should remain constant and independent of its position relative to the pixel structure.*

5.4. COMPUTATIONAL ACCURACY OF INTENSITY

A spatial filter must be implemented in a manner that produces transitional-pixel intensities to the required degree of accuracy. There is no established solution because the matter is subjective and because it also depends on a number of variables. The determination of the required accuracy is important because it determines the number of subpixels or quanta of area. In addition, to meet accuracy requirements the word

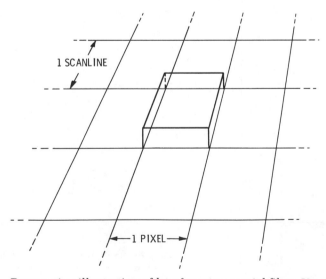

Figure 5.9. Perspective illustration of box function spatial filter. Vertical dimension is filter value.

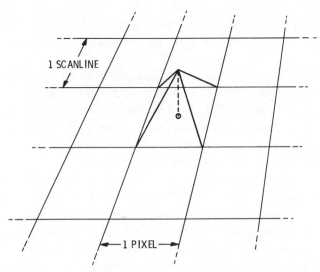

Figure 5.10. Perspective illustration of pyramid function spatial filter spanning a single pixel.

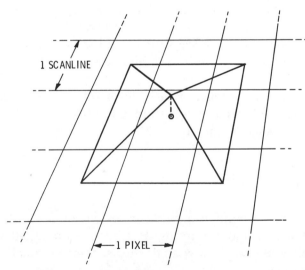

Figure 5.11. Perspective illustration of pyramid spatial filter spanning 2 × 2 pixels. Note that this filter spans both fields.

lengths used for intensities must be determined, and this in turn may govern whether computational circuits or table lookup methods are used for the implementation.

Both contrast and brightness significantly influence accuracy requirements. The greater these are, the greater is the required accuracy. This is not surprising since it is well known that the human visual system is more sensitive to flicker as brightness increases. Thus night visual systems may have acceptable aliasing properties with only two bits of computational accuracy, but more accuracy is certainly needed for day or dusk systems.

Accuracy requirements are also a function of pixel size. The smaller the pixel (i.e., its angular subtend at the eye), the less accuracy is required since the eye's limited resolution results in an attenuation of the intensity difference of two adjacent pixels. On the other hand, it has been hypothesized, but not proven, that aliasing is more of a problem in the eye's periphery than one may expect from its resolving power. Although resolution decreases sharply toward the periphery, flicker and motion sensitivity increase.

Color and luminance also have significant effects on aliasing. In the absence of spatial filtering, strong aliasing is detected when an edge separates light and dark areas of the same color. However, aliasing is hardly noticeable between two areas of different color which have the same luminous intensity (e.g., adjacent red and green faces of the same intensity). This is not surprising because it is well known that the eye has a much higher resolving capability for luminance contrast than for color contrast.

Because of the large number of variables involved, the chosen number of subpixels per pixel varies widely from one system to another. In practical systems, this range is from 4 to 64.

5.5. TEMPORAL EFFECTS

The effects of temporal undersampling are in general not as disturbing as the effects of spatial undersampling. However, temporal effects are not nearly as well understood as spatial effects; their elimination is more difficult.

Perhaps the least understood anomaly is the *interlace effect*. When an object shown on a CRT moves up or down the screen, it will appear to break up into a series of parallel bands, as if every other field were missing. The effect is most pronounced when an object travels at a rate of one scan line per field time. This problem is particularly obvious for large,

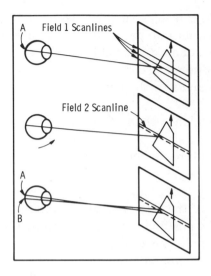

Figure 5.12. Illustration of the interlace effect.

evenly illuminated faces. But it also manifests itself as a breakup of narrow stripes.

Unlike spatial aliasing, this temporal effect is present in all interlaced television, not just in computer-generated images. On commercial TV programs it is most noticeable on long narrow lines, such as found on tennis courts and football fields. The problem is best explained by illustration; see Figure 5.12.

In Figure 5.12 the face is being painted by a series of scan lines in field 1, but since it is an interlaced system, only every other scan line appears on this field. The image of one of these scan lines falls on point A of the retina. Next, consider field 2, normally displayed $\frac{1}{60}$ of a second later. If the object is moving up the screen at a rate of one scan line per field time, it will have moved up one scan line. The eye, however, will follow the object as defined by its outer boundaries. The eye will therefore rotate, so that point A on the retina will be looking at a place one scan line above the spot where it was previously looking. However, this is exactly the place where a scan line of field 2 is now being painted. Consequently point A on the retina will be illuminated by a scan line of each field. Conversely, point B on the retina, corresponding to one scan line below, will find itself never illuminated by a scan line, so long as the eye continues to track the object. The result is that the object appears to be made up of only every other scan line.

The interlace effect has a more serious consequence than just appearing to halve the number of scan lines. As an example, consider a small face, such as might represent a runway marking. This face may appear only on a single scan line. It would move down the screen as the pilot "lands" the plane. If this face moves at a rate of one scan line per field time, it may completely disappear from view, because whenever the field consisting of the odd scan lines is shown, the face's position may correspond to an even scan line. Conversely, when the even scan lines are displayed, its position may be odd.

Obviously, it's only an unlucky coincidence if the face's motion is exactly synchronous with the field rate. It is also unlucky if the speed of the face is close to one scan line per field time. When this happens, the face will alternately blink on and off.

In the above example we assumed that the position of the face was calculated every field time. The problem of the face alternately blinking on and off can be solved by calculating the position of the face only once per frame time. While this overcomes the interlace effect, it creates a new problem, which we describe below as the frame rate update effect.

Another solution to the interlace effect is to use a wide spatial filter that scans two pixels and two scan lines, as shown in Figure 5.11. This solution has two drawbacks: (1) it reduces resolution and (2) it requires a memory with a capacity of at least one field.

Since the interlace effect is caused by the motion of scene parts, it disappears when the scene is frozen. This disappearance is not instantaneous because the eye continues to track the moving object for a fraction of a second after it actually stops moving.

One obvious solution to the interlace effect is to use a noninterlaced system. However, this approach is not economical since it requires a doubling of the effective bandwidth and computation rate.

Another anomaly closely related to the interlace effect results from sampling at the frame rate instead of the field rate. In some early CIG systems the position of each edge was updated at the frame rate. This gives rise to the *frame rate update effect*. To understand this effect, consider Figure 5.13 and assume that a narrow line, such as a runway stripe, is moving horizontally toward the right. At the start of field 1 it would be at position A. At the beginning of field 2 it would be at position B. If the position of the edge is computed at the field rate, the CRT will contain the information as shown in Figure 5.13. To the eye that tracks the motion of the stripe, positions A and B will overlap on the retina, and consequently only a single stripe will be visible. Now consider the case when the position of the stripe is recomputed only once per frame time. For this case the stripe is in position A for both fields 1 and 2. If the eye is tracking the stripe at a constant speed, there will appear to be two stripes on the retina, displaced by a distance D, which is the product of the velocity of

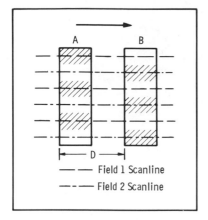

Figure 5.13.   The frame rate update effect.

the stripe and the field interval ($\frac{1}{60}$ second). Each stripe of this double-stripe image will appear to be at reduced contrast.

A less serious anomaly is the *stroboscopic effect*. It will be explained by example. Consider a propeller that spins so rapidly that it appears as a blur to the eye. On a digitally generated display, the simulation of this propeller may appear to be stopped, exactly as the actual propeller would appear under a strobe light. This stroboscopic effect can be avoided by using a special data-base primitive: the semitransparent face. To simulate a rotating propeller, a circular face would be required. But even this solution does not always work. The revolutions of helicopter blades vary from speeds where the blade is clearly visible to speeds where only a blur can be seen. Depicting the blade's transition from one speed to another is a difficult problem.

5.6.   CONCLUSION

CIG technology has now progressed to a state where the causes of the various aliasing effects are fairly well understood. Algorithms are known for suppressing these effects. The challenge is now to find economical solutions, since the mathematically exact solutions are too expensive to implement. These approximate solutions must be based on a good under-standing of human perception, because the ultimate judge of the accept-ability of an image is the observer. Any deviation from the mathematically exact solutions must be based upon experiments in perception.

6 DATA-BASE DESIGN

BRUCE J. SCHACHTER

6.1. INTRODUCTION

The three main components of any (daytime) scene that a pilot sees are terrain, culture, and 3-D objects. A scene model is a specification of the way in which these components are stored on a data-base disk. The representation for the entire geographic region of interest is called the visual data base for the region. A data base must be efficient to create, efficient to store, easy to modify, and in a suitable form for the algorithms that will process it under a particular CIG architecture. It is the visual data base that drives the hardware. When a pilot flies outside the modeled area, the image generator has nothing to display, except possibly some default pattern.

The ground features that a pilot sees in a simulated scene are modeled to be of the same size, shape, location, color, and sometimes texture as their real-world counterparts. This is especially important in and around airports and other areas of special interest. The simulated imagery should be faithful enough to actual conditions to allow the pilot to fly by "visual reference." Commercial aircraft fly between preset locations over a fixed flight path. Military aircraft must be capable of traveling over a large territory (called the gaming area) at varying altitudes and speeds. Data bases for military simulators are generally more complex and contain more special features (e.g., missiles, smoke, flack) than those for civilian aircraft.

6.2. REPRESENTATION OF TERRAIN

In the real world, terrain is a continuous surface. Thus even a small patch of ground could be represented by an infinite number of elevation points. Since it is not possible to depict the land surface exactly, the objective is to obtain a satisfactory representation, which minimizes the effort required to develop, store, and display the data base.

One source of data, used by U.S. manufacturers, is the Defense Mapping Agency's terrain and culture files (Figure 6.1). A terrain file is an array of elevation values for a region of the earth. Since an elevation array consists of only the altitude of the surface at each sample point, geographic locations are determined by grid spacing, and are implicit in the sequential positions of the altitude values within the storage array. One advantage of this method of storage is that the neighbors of a sample point are easily located. The principal disadvantage of a grid is the certainty of redundancy, since the grid must be sufficiently dense to portray the smallest terrain feature of interest. To improve the resolution by a factor of n requires that the grid spacing be decreased by this factor, increasing the number of sample points by a factor of n^2. Smooth subareas then contain far more sample points than are required to portray them. Other problems arise when displaying an array data base directly. When shown in perspective, areas close to the viewpoint will have a blocky appearance. For regions close to the horizon, a very large number of sample points will have to be processed to obtain the color assignment for a single pixel. The usual solution to this problem is to place a false horizon nearer to the viewpoint than the actual horizon. Another possible approach would be to use a coarser sampling of the data base toward the horizon. This would suggest the use of a quad-tree data structure. No organization has successfully built a visual flight simulator using a grid data base; however, several are now trying.

Contour lines represent another way to sample and store the land surface. The elevations of contours are fixed by sea level and the contour

Data Base	Terrain Data, Resolution	Culture Data, Equivalent Map Scale	Coverage
Level I	3 arc seconds	1:250,000 to 1:100,000	Worldwide
Level II	1 arc second	1:50,000 to 1:25,000	Local regions
Level III	less than 1 arc second	better than 1:25,000	Special areas

Figure 6.1. Defense Mapping Agency Data-base scale and coverage.

intervals, and thus are not derived directly from the important surface features of the terrain. Contour maps are available for many geographic areas. They can be easily input to the computer via a digitizing tablet or automated techniques. The usual approach is to store them in chain coded form. Contour lines are not used directly for display by a visual simulator, but may occasionally serve as an input source or as an intermediate representation during data-base development.

Another approach to storing a terrain surface is the curvilinear surface patch. Here specific mathematical functions are developed to describe each patch. This usually involves fitting low-order polynomial functions of two variables to small terrain areas. In a geophysical context, Mark [MARK75, MARK79] concludes that the polynomial patch is not an appropriate medium for terrain representation. The polynomial patch does not relate directly to the phenomenon of interest (i.e., the earth's topography—mountain peaks, ridge lines, etc.), is not convenient for computer storage, and is not ideal for rapid display. Patches may be useful models of average quantities, but cannot accommodate slope discontinuities or local roughness changes conveniently, without being redundant over much of the modeled area. Yan [YAN80], of the Singer Company, evaluates a number of schemes of this type popular in non-real-time computer graphics, and concludes that none are suitable for CIG. A group [SOLA81] at Honeywell reaches an opposite conclusion.

One common terrain representation scheme, used since GE's earliest models, treats the world as flat, except for mountains, which are modeled as pyramids and placed onto the level ground. The obvious rationalization is that a pilot is not particularly concerned about valleys, but must avoid mountain tops. This thought line holds up better for commercial aircraft simulators than for those for high-performance military aircraft in which a pilot must practice nap-of-the-earth (ground hugging) flight. The pyramid/plane approach to terrain representation is particularly appropriate for low-cost civilian systems. It simplifies many other aspects of system design. For example, texture, 3-D objects, and shadows can be much more easily placed onto flat ground than on any other type of surface form.

Terrain points are *surface specific* if they provide more information about the topography than just that given by their coordinates. Surface specific points require more storage per point than grid points, since all three coordinates must be explicitly specified. These types of points can be obtained from grid data bases by applying digital filters which extract local maxima, minima, and saddle points. Ridge-line segments can be extracted by edge detectors. Such filters are common in computer image processing. Surface specific points can be joined together to form a triangular network of faces, such that the ridge lines will lie on the edges of the triangulation [LEE80]. These faces in aggregate form a piecewise planar approximation to the earth's relief. Such a planar faceted representation is particularly convenient for processing, storage, and display. Most sophisticated CIG systems use a triangular faceted terrain model. A triangular model can be made hierarchical. At each successively higher level of the hierarchy, an area of terrain is represented by a cluster of smaller triangles. A hierarchical data base must be stored with pointers between levels so that as the pilot changes altitude, the displayed levels of detail change accordingly. Even when the aircraft's altitude is held steady, coarser levels of detail must be displayed toward the horizon. GE has developed several schemes of this type, the details of which are proprietary. One drawback of piecewise planar surfaces is that they are discontinuous at edges. This produces an angular appearance and creates forbidden zones upon which 3-D objects cannot be placed.

Representational validity is of obvious importance to ensure the integrity of the ground surface. An invalid description may cause a "crash" in the data-base development software; or if it gets into the CIG system, it may produce a nonsense surface, streaks, or mountains popping in and out of view—all of which may lead to a trainer pilot "crash."

To completely define a triangular terrain surface requires not only a geometry to specify the dimensions and locations of its constituent parts, but also a topology of the adjacency relations between respective parts. The geometric description involves data, while the topological description involves structure (which in practice involves the way data are organized in computer storage). Without both types of descriptions, the shape of a surface is not completely specified, and valid processing is not possible.

A CIG's on-line storage cannot hold the entire data base for a gaming area in its memory at once. Therefore the modeled terrain surface is stored on disk in blocks. As a pilot approaches a new geographic area, the block representing it is retrieved and placed into on-line storage.

The following set of conditions must be satisfied for geometric validity of a triangular terrain surface:

1. Each vertex must be represented by three numeric values.
2. Edges must be disjoint or intersect at a common vertex.
3. Faces must be disjoint or intersect at a common edge or vertex.

4. Vertices on the common border of adjacent terrain blocks must coincide.

Another set of conditions must be met for topological validity.

5. Each face must have precisely three edges.
6. Each edge must have precisely two vertices.
7. Each nonborderline edge in a block must belong to two faces, while each borderline edge in a block must belong to one face within the block.
8. Each vertex in a block must belong to three or more faces if it is not on a border line, two or more faces if it is on a border line, one or more faces if it is a corner point.

When terrain is modeled hierarchically, additional sets of consistency conditions are required.

6.3. REPRESENTATION OF CULTURE

In the terminology of the industry, "culture" refers to man-made and ecological surface features. Typical features are lakes, rivers, forests, vineyards, orchards, swamps, mud flats, permafrost, farmland, urban areas, desert, and roads. Terrain data specifies the topography of the land, while culture indicates its color and texture.

The Defense Mapping Agency's culture files consist mainly of the polygonal borders of culture features, together with encoded descriptions of the contents of the polygons. A single Defense Mapping Agency culture polygon may have several thousand vertices. This is more data than a CIG system can process. During data-base development, techniques like those given by Pavlidis [PAVL77] are required to reduce the number of vertices, with as little distortion in shape and size as possible. (Accuracy requirements for both terrain and culture are often specified by contract.) Each polygon may be represented in the data base at quite a few different levels of detail, with pointers between successive representations.

Culture data can also be obtained from maps and aerial photographs.

Suppose that a triangular terrain representation is used. In order to color the terrain surface, each culture polygon of a particular level of detail must be intersected with the triangular network of the same level of detail. Each polygon must then be broken up into subpolygons, such that no subpolygon crosses an edge of the triangulation. Culture fragments are often partitioned further into convex components [SCHA78], as is required by the algorithms implemented in most CIG systems.

Culture polygons must be validated at each stage of their representation during the data-base development process. Most importantly, polygons must be "simple." That is, edges must be disjoint, except for adjacent edges which can intersect only once—at their common vertex. Other restrictions also usually need to be met. Vertices should not be duplicated. Adjacent edges should not be colinear. Polygons should not have dangling edges or stranded vertices. Several polygons violating these conditions are shown in Figure 6.2a.

Due to system limitations, there are always additional restrictions involving the total number of vertices, edges, and faces allowed within a data block. If these conditions are not met during the initial creation of a data base, a correction can be made by postprocessing. An example is shown in Figure 6.2b.

Another approach to placing culture onto a triangular faceted surface is to use a Voronoi mosaic, constructed as follows. During data-base development, a small number of points (Voronoi nuclei) are placed onto each triangle. Each of these nuclei defines a convex cell, consisting of all points on the triangle nearer to it than to any other nucleus. A particular culture type is associated with each nucleus. When a triangular face is displayed, each spot on the face is assigned the color associated with the nearest (in terms of the plane of the triangle in the original 3-D space) Voronoi nu-

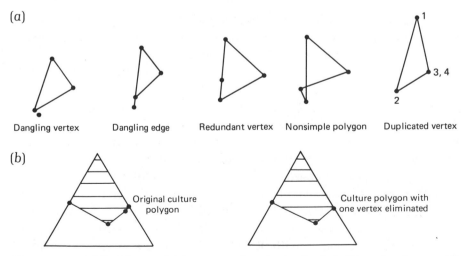

Figure 6.2.   (a) Problems which commonly arise in the definition of polygons. (b) Data-base reduction by post-processing.

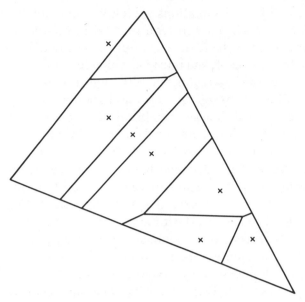

Figure 6.3. Representation of the cultural content of a terrain triangle by a Voronoi mosaic. The Voronoi points are denoted by x. Each cell consists of the region of the triangle closer to its Voronoi point than to any of the other Voronoi points.

cleus. Thus only one point is required to specify an entire culture polygon. An example is shown in Figure 6.3.

6.4. REPRESENTATION OF 3-D OBJECTS

Locations and descriptions of 3-D objects can be obtained from Defense Mapping Agency tapes, maps, charts, drawings, photographs, and airport blueprints. To the author's knowledge, the only category of solids that have been used thus far in CIG systems is polyhedra (mainly convex), although GE [BUNK77c] and possibly Singer [YAN79] appear to have developed the technology to generate quadric objects (ellipsoids, cones, and cylinders).

A number of schemes are available for modeling geometric solids. In classical Cartesian geometry, a polyhedron is usually represented by a set of faces, a face by a set of edges, an edge by a pair of vertices, and a vertex by a point in 3-D space. However, an object can also be represented by a set of edges or vertices, a face by a string of vertices, an edge by the intersection of faces, and a vertex by the intersection of edges or faces.

Storing all possible representations is highly redundant. However, different algorithms in a system will require data in different forms. It is not good enough for data to be in the right form somewhere in the system, but more precisely, an item of data must be available to those system modules that require it when they require it. Although it is possible to transform data back and forth between one form and another, this is the last thing that is desired in a real-time system. In practice, specific redundant information accumulated off-line during data-base development is required to make real-time processing possible. All CIG systems are designed around a predefined tradeoff point between processing and storage capacities. Geometric representations, data structures, and on-line storage size must be specified as an integral part of system definition. Consider several examples of these concepts. (1) Although surface normals are not required to define a polyhedron unambiguously, it is often more economical to store them than to compute them on-line. Surface normals are used in sunshading and hidden-surface calculations. (2) Other redundant information stored often involves adjacency relations between faces, edges, and vertices. The availability of such data avoids expensive searches. (3) CIG algorithms can sometimes be put into simpler form by placing restrictions on the locations of objects; for example, by not allowing clouds or low-flying aircraft (other than owncraft) to pass below the peak of the highest mountain. Restrictions may also be placed on the use of shadows.

When 3-D data are created off-line, some assurance is needed that they are correct. It is not feasible to load the data into the CIG and inspect them from every possible altitude and view direction. Topological relations must satisfy a number of consistency conditions.

1. Each edge must join exactly two vertices and two faces.
2. Each face must be surrounded by an equal number (≥ 3) of faces and edges.
3. Each vertex must be surrounded by an equal number (≥ 3) of faces and edges.
4. For a convex polyhedron, the number of vertices, faces, and edges must satisfy Euler's equation $V + F - E = 2$.

A general strategy for reducing the storage requirements of object data is to exploit the redundancies within the data. Objects that are similar and repeated throughout the data base may be stored on-line once in common form and retrieved when needed. This inherently involves some additional on-line computation to prepare each instance of a generic item. The alternatives of which information to store and which to compute are important, but tradeoffs are very hard to analyze. Alternative collections of redundant information must be identified, the storage costs of each determined, the costs of alternative computation sequences estimated, and a determination made that the upper bound on computation time will not be violated.

Objects are often stored at a number of levels of detail. This implies a requirement for pointers between levels of detail and switching ranges indicating when to replace or blend particular levels of detail.

Three experimental approaches to representing solids are described next.

Octree encoding [DOCT81] is a hierarchical representation scheme for solids. It has been used at Rensselaer Polytechnic Institute in the real-time nonperspective projection of 3-D space arrays. An octree data structure is a directed graph of nodes (Figure 6.4a). Each node contains a list of 8

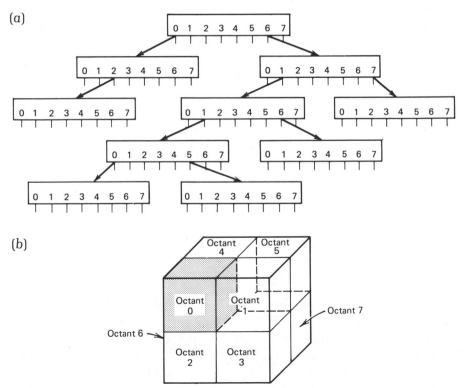

Figure 6.4. (a) An octree is a directed graph composed of nodes. (b) Octree nodes contain *eight* data elements which correspond to the octants of a region in space. Shaded area covers one octant.

elements corresponding to octants of a region of space (Figure 6.4b). A flag in each data element indicates whether or not the associated octant is homogeneous. When a flag indicates that a particular octant is homogeneous, the remainder of the data element is taken as the associated volume element's color. Alternatively, the data element in a heterogeneous octant contains a pointer to another node which subdivides the region. Empty regions are represented by a volume element filled with special values indicating a void.

Another approach to representing a solid is the *procedural, syntactic,* or *algorithmic model*. Instead of storing a building or a tree by all the data points that describe it, rules for generating the objects' data points are stored. Consider the problem of a pilot flying over a forest. If pilots flew low enough they might see individual leaves of the trees (probably just before they crashed). Clearly a data base cannot store a description of every leaf of every tree in the forest. However, an algorithm which generates trees to varying levels of hierarchy could be used. When the pilot is far from a given tree, the algorithm is executed in its most basic form to generate a single polyhedron to represent the tree. As the pilot gets closer to the tree, the algorithm is executed further to generate several leaf blobs. At nearer ranges some branches and smaller leaf blobs could be developed and shown. Some randomness can be introduced into this process to give each tree in the forest a different appearance. But upon closer examination, although the procedural model approach may make good marketing copy, it has little practical value in CIG. A generic tree can be more economically stored and displayed at several levels of detail (with blending between levels) than generated from a procedural model.

The simplest of the curved surfaces are the *quadric surfaces*. In a Cartesian coordinate system a quadric surface is the locus of the general second-order equation

$$s(x, y, z) = a_1x^2 + a_2y^2 + a_3z^2 + a_4xy + a_5yz + a_6xz$$
$$+ a_7x + a_8y + a_9z + a_{10}$$

where the a_i are all real numbers. The surface degenerates to a plane when $a_1, a_2, \ldots, a_6$ are all zero. A polyhedron can be conveniently modeled in terms of its vertices, edges, and faces. To specify a quadric object unambiguously is not such a simple matter. A complete specification must contain the equivalent of the following [WOON70]:

1. The equations defining each component surface of the object
2. The polarity of each component surface (i.e., an indication as to which of the two sides of a surface is on the outside of the object)

3. The bounds of each component surface (i.e., a Boolean combination of inequalities specifying exactly how the component surface is bounded)

Quadric objects are so simple and common that they can readily be conceived of by a data-base modeler. Familiar shapes include the ellipsoid (one surface), quadric cone (two surfaces), and capped cylinder (three surfaces). In training simulators, quadric objects could be used to represent water towers, trees, missiles, silos, and clouds. However, since aesthetics is not a concern in CIG, these objects could just as well be built from planar faces (possibly with curved-surface shading in display). In certain instances, such as displaying a rotating rocket, too much smoothness in shading defeats the desired visual effect. It is for these reasons that even though the technology to display quadric surfaces has been developed in the CIG industry, no company has put much effort into integrating a quadric object generator into an overall system design.

6.5. A DATA-BASE DEVELOPMENT AND DISPLAY FACILITY

A visual data base is a high-level mathematical model of a region of the real world. It is created through the manual and automatic processing of the available source material, which may include Defense Mapping Agency tapes, maps, drawings, airport blueprints, aerial photographs, etc. Automatic processing is required to prepare the bulk of the data base, with manual techniques reserved for areas of special interest. Section 6.5.1 describes the organization of a suggested system for converting the source material into a visual data base. A block diagram of the system hardware units is given in Section 6.5.5.

6.5.1. Digital Data-Base Development System: System Tasks

The data-base development system will perform four primary tasks, as illustrated in Figure 6.5.

6.5.1.1. *Intermediate Data-Base Construction*

This operation is performed by routines which accept data from different sources and generate intermediate data bases from them. In order to maintain system efficiency and flexibility, the operation of each of the processing routines should be well defined and separate from the others. The files

148

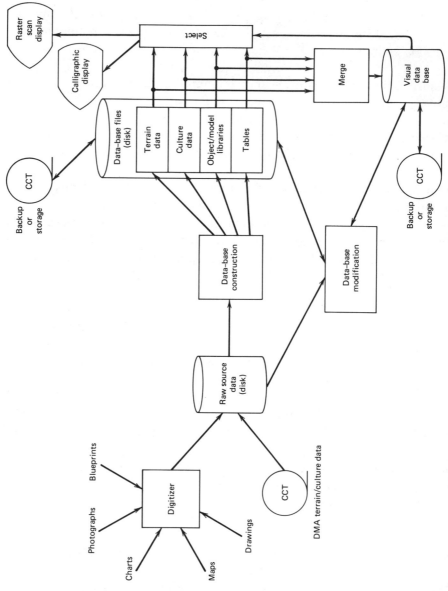

Figure 6.5. Possible data-base development system. Flow diagram. (CCT = computer compatible tape.)

produced by these routines are intermediate files which will be formatted and combined in whole or in part into a final visual data-base file. Some of the subtasks involved in this operation are described below.

A.   Terrain Data-Base Development.   A terrain data base will consist of a network of triangles. The source data will be Defense Mapping Agency digital terrain files, contour maps, and/or surface specific points. Routines can be developed to automatically fit a triangular faceted surface to digital terrain arrays. Contour maps can be input to the computer by mounting them on a digitizing tablet and having the operator trace the contour lines with a digitizing stylus. After each contour line is entered, the operator will type in its elevation. Software routines can be developed to automatically construct a triangular network from a contour map.

Maps, drawings, and aerial photographs can also be used as data sources. The operator will mount and register a data sheet onto a digitizing tablet, and then point to specific terrain points with the stylus and enter their elevations via keyboard. Ridge segments will be input by their endpoint pairs. A triangulation will then be automatically formed over these points and segments.

B.   Culture Data-Base Development.   The bulk of culture data will be input to the computer from Defense Mapping Agency culture tapes. Cultural information for areas of special interest will be obtained from maps, charts, drawings, and photographs. This source material will be mounted on the digitizing tablet, and the polygonal culture areas traced with a stylus. The operator will then type in the required descriptive parameters.

C.   Object/Model Data-Base Development.   The data-base development system should have the capability to generate and maintain object and model libraries.

An *object library* consists of a directory accessible accumulation of data sets, where each data set completely defines a 3-D object.

A *model library*, like an object library, consists of a directory accessible accumulation of data sets, where each data set shall be referred to as a model. The difference between object and model libraries is that an object library contains one-of-a-kind objects (e.g., the control tower at Kennedy Airport), whereas a model library contains standard generic objects (e.g., pine trees, houses, or agricultural sheds). A model will be defined only once. There may, however, be many pointers to the same model distributed throughout the visual data base. Each pointer might have an associated set of parameters (e.g., color, rotation, scale). During data-base development, any item from the object library should be transferable to the model library by a simple command.

D.   Table Entry.   Several tabulated data sets are required. Tables will contain such information as the parameters governing the color and texture of scene components. For example, a culture polygon may have a code indicating that it represents a deciduous forest. This code will be a pointer to table entries defining the color and texture of the forest. An important part of the visual data-base development process is the definition, generation, and modification of tabulated data.

Several alternate tables may be available for the same scene. They will allow an instructor to display the scene as it would be seen at different times of day (e.g., at midnight or at sunset) or on different sensor types (e.g., FLIR, LLLTV).

6.5.1.2.   Data-Base Modification

Several intermediate files will be created during data-base development. In order to correct deficiencies noted during display, or to add to the intermediate data bases, each intermediate terrain, culture, or parameter file should be capable of being modified.

6.5.1.3.   Data-Base Merging

The visual data base will be produced by merging the following intermediate data types: (1) triangular terrain network, (2) polygonal culture data, (3) object/model libraries, and (4) tabulated data. The data-base development system operator will type in the names of the files to be merged, then the merging process will be automatic. The merging routines will inform the operator of any conflicts in data definition. A typical conflict will be an attempt to place an object onto the edge of a terrain triangle.

6.5.1.4.   (Non-Real-Time) Data-Base Display

The data-base modeler requires the ability to inspect the assembled data. The data-base development process produces several different data types. The display system should be capable of displaying each intermediate data type, as well as the final visual data base. This implies that the graphic equipment includes both calligraphic (also called vector or stroke writing) and raster scan modes. A calligraphic system will provide a quick "wire frame" drawing. A raster scan system will be slower, but will allow the visualization of a complete sun shaded scene, with haze and other special effects included. The raster scan display software may be an emulator of the CIG algorithms.

In order to reduce the burden on the operator, the actual display commands should be independent of data types. The entered command routine should cue the operator to supply required parameters. This implies the existence of data formatting and conversion routines to serve as an interface between the display commands and the data.

6.5.2. Interactive Data-Base Development and Display Commands

Each of the four data-base development and display tasks is accomplished by a number of commands. The system operator will type in a command at the operator's console. Then the operator will be querried by the system or will be asked to perform certain tasks. If the operator attempts something illegal (e.g., enters data out of range), an error message will be printed and the command exited. A block diagram showing the organization of system commands and utility routines is given in Figure 6.6.

6.5.3. Utility Routines

A number of utility routines are required to support the visual data-base development task. These include:

1. Operator interfaces
2. Device drivers
    a. Calligraphic
    b. Raster scan
    c. Digitizing tablet
3. Data handlers
    a. Data formatting and manipulation routines
    b. File managers
4. Command files

All of the above software modules should be subordinate to the system executive. This will allow a top-down structured software design, as well as permit the development of a controllable, flexible, expandable system.

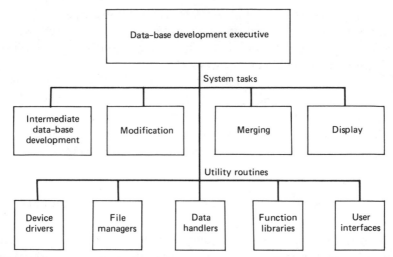

Figure 6.6. Organization of interactive commands and utility routines.

Calls to utility routines should be transparent to the system operator. The system executive will enable the operator to communicate with a general-purpose computer's operating system and the data-base development software only through the defined interactive command structure.

6.5.4. Portability and Standardization

For advanced CIG systems, the CIG, contracted visual data bases, data-base development software, support software, host computers, peripherals, graphic hardware, and documentation are usually sold as a package. For reasons relating to the multiplicity of contracts and the competitive nature of the marketplace, portability and standardization are not goals in the CIG industry.

6.5.5. System Hardware

The recommended data-base development system is composed of off-the-shelf equipment configured as shown in Figure 6.7. The two major subsystems are the computer and its peripherals and the graphic workstation.

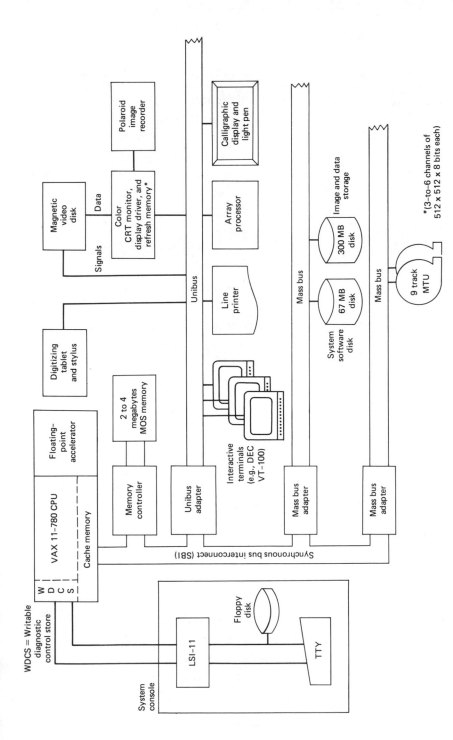

Figure 6.7. A data-base development facility.

153

These are comprised as follows:

Computer Subsystem	Graphic Workstation
1 medium size, 32-bit computer (with 2 to 4 megabytes of core storage)	1 digitizing tablet and stylus
1 array processor	1 color CRT monitor (with 3 to 6 channels of refresh memory and display driver)
1 line printer (with dot matrix image printing capabilities)	1 monochromatic CRT (with refresh memory)
2 disk drives (one 67 megabyte and one 300 megabyte)	1 calligraphic display and light pen
2 nine-track magnetic tape units	1 8 × 10 inch Polaroid film image recorder
1 system console	1 magnetic video disk
1 to 3 interactive terminals	

The Digital Equipment Co. VAX computer or equivalent medium-scale mainframe is recommended. Core and storage capacities are based upon the requirements of the image storage and display tasks.

7 GENERATION OF SPECIAL EFFECTS

BRUCE J. SCHACHTER

7.1. INTRODUCTION

A flight simulator pays for itself if aircraft fuel and maintenance costs are reduced significantly during normal flight training. A somewhat different reason for using a simulator is to perform tasks which are too difficult or dangerous to undertake in an actual aircraft. Simulating conditions of this type often involves the generation of special effects.

Important among these effects are adverse weather conditions. These include the visual effects of ground fog, haze, scud and storm clouds, halos around airport lights, and horizon glow. The sounds of wind and thunder and the effects of wind on aircraft dynamics may also be simulated.

Keeping a fighter pilot air-superior requires his practice of emergency procedures and combat maneuvers. Typical emergency conditions are the failure of landing and taxi lights and various types of mechanical failures. Combat practice includes dogfighting in two-cockpit simulators, which involves attack and evasive maneuvers. The missiles that a pilot would fire in an actual kill-or-be-killed dogfight are too expensive to be used extensively in training. Air Force pilots often go through their entire careers without firing a single real missile, while their Navy counterparts might fire a missile every couple of years. The least expensive missiles for dogfighting are the heat-seeking Sidewinders, which cost $60,000 a piece. The Navy's Phoenix air-to-air missiles cost about $2 million each; the radar-directed Sparrows, about $150,000 each. Missiles can, of course, be "fired" one after the other in a simulator, with no worry as to cost.

Combat pilots must also practice nap-of-the-earth (ground hugging) flight. A simulated scene must have sufficient detail (texture) to support such flight. If pilots cannot obtain enough visual cues from the simulated scene to maneuver their aircraft just above the ground, they will continually crash into it, making the training sessions worthless.

7.2. TEXTURE

When pilots fly over terrestrial landscapes, they see patchworks of different plant species and land uses. Cities, swamps, deserts, oceans, forests, orchards, and farmland all have distinctive variegation—or texture (Figure 7.1). These textures may be divided into two basic categories, natural and man-made. The first category consists of very random patterns, such as those resulting from natural phenomena. The second category includes patterns caused by human intervention, such as urban, suburban, industrial, farmland, runway surface, brick wall. These man-made textures often have a rectilinear grid structure.

One good model for the first category of textures is the Gaussian random field. A pattern of this type can be produced by a sum of long-crested narrow-band noise waveforms [SCHA80a], designated by $n(\cdot)$. A texture t is defined by the equation

$$t(\eta_1, \eta_2) = \mu \sum_{i=1}^{k} B_i n(u_i \eta_1 + v_i \eta_2 + \phi_i), \qquad k \leq 3$$

where η_1 and η_2 are the axes of the coordinate system, the B_i are amplitude modulators, the ϕ_i are phase shifts, and μ is the background color vector. The mean angular frequency of a waveform in a direction perpendicular to the crestfront is $\omega = (u_i^2 + v_i^2)^{\frac{1}{2}}$. The angle of the ith long-crested wave is $\theta_i = \tan^{-1}(v_i/u_i)$.

The appearance of a texture of this type can vary quite widely with suitable control of the parameters of the model. Two long-crested waves 90° apart will produce a texture with a rectilinear microstructure, which may be appropriate for simulating an orchard. Three waveforms, 60° apart, will produce a texture with an underlying hexagonal structure, which may be useful for depicting a forest. A single high-frequency waveform will produce a texture with long narrow rows, similar to a plowed field (Figure 7.2).

This texture model is particularly appropriate for real-time perspective display because its generative equation is linear in the values of the axes of the coordinate system [BUNK77c].

A different model is needed for simulating the more regular man-made patterns. An important feature of many of these patterns is roads which crisscross background regions and in some sense have priority over them. These textures can be modeled by the equation [SCHA80c]

$$t(\eta_1, \eta_2) = \mu \sum_{i=1}^{2} P[p_1(\eta_1), p_2(\eta_2)] f_i(\eta_i)$$

where P is the priority function defined as follows:

$$P[p_1(\eta_1), p_2(\eta_2)] = \begin{cases} \frac{1}{2} & \text{if and only if } p_1(\eta_1) = p_2(\eta_2) = 0 \\ \delta_{i,1} & \text{if and only if } p_1(\eta_1) \geq p_2(\eta_2) \text{ and } p_1(\eta_1) > 0 \\ \delta_{i,2} & \text{if and only if } p_2(\eta_2) > p_1(\eta_1) \end{cases}$$

$\delta_{i,j}$ being the Kronecker delta. A texture produced by this equation is shown in Figure 7.3.

For these man-made textures it is up to the data-base modeler to develop functions f_i and p_i to produce the desired patterns. This can be easily done through the use of an interactive computer graphic system. Again, note that this texturing equation is linear in the values of the coordinate system.

One enhancement that can be readily accomplished in hardware is the replacement of a generated color intensity by a function of it. This can be done rapidly and inexpensively by the use of a lookup table. For example, a 256-entry lookup table can be used to map a computed 8-bit color intensity to another value. One application of this mapping is the transformation of unimodal textures to bimodality (Figure 7.4).

It is clear that the scale to which a texture is displayed must change along with a pilot's changing altitude. It should also be clear that even when the altitude is held steady, the component elements of the texture must be made smaller toward the horizon. Consider a large texture cell below the aircraft. An identically sized cell near the horizon may cover but a single pixel. Not only could such undersampling of a texture create serious aliasing problems, but also a tremendous amount of processing would be required to determine a color assignment for this single pixel.

(a)

(b)

Figure 7.1. Aerial photographs showing some different textures. (a) Forest, (b) Farmland.

Figure 7.1. (c) Suburban. (d) Orchard.

Figure 7.2. Scene produced by the GE B-52 visual simulator showing the use of a long-crested sinusoid to depict a plowed field.

Figure 7.3. Simulated city texture at three levels of detail, without blending between levels of detail (produced by software).

Figure 7.4.   Bimodal swamp texture produced by mapping a unimodal Gaussian random field formed by the sum of three long-crested narrow-band noise waves (produced by software).

One solution is to display textures at a number of levels of detail. GE's fourth-generation systems generate textures at ten levels of detail. To reduce aliasing problems, succeedingly lower levels of detail are given lower intensity ranges. That is, the means of textured surfaces remain fixed toward the horizon, but the variances are reduced.

The level of detail that an image point receives must therefore be a function of the distance between the surface point and the view point. The border between two levels of detail is an arc which travels across the ground at a fixed distance from the pilot. If care is not taken, this arc will look like a shock wave rippling across the earth. GE's systems prevent this by gradually blending one level of detail into the next.

Another type of undersampling occurs when a textured surface becomes nearly parallel to the view line. This condition can be handled by having the image generation hardware check for it and reduce texture levels of detail accordingly.

7.3.   CLOUDS

Cumulus cloud layers can be simulated by a concatenation of cloud groups. A cloud group may consist of about 75 sunshaded ellipsoids confined to a circular envelope (as viewed from above). The sizes and shapes of these simulated clouds should roughly correspond to that of real clouds. An example is shown in Figure 7.5. The cloud layer elevation

Figure 7.5.   Cloud layer constructed from ellipsoids.

and percent coverage should be controllable by the instructor at the start
of a training session.

Data describing cloud groups can be stored on the visual data-base disk.
Seven cloud groups of the instructor-specified percent coverage can be
loaded into on-line core at the start of a training session. The center cloud
group should initially be placed directly above owncraft (the pilot's own
aircraft) (Figure 7.6). We will say that pilots are traveling within the center
cloud group region of coverage if they are within it, above it, or below it.
Once a training session starts, not only will owncraft move, but the clouds
will drift parallel to the earth's surface, according to an instructor-
programmed wind speed and direction. The position of owncraft relative
to the center cloud group will be monitored. Once owncraft leaves the
center cloud group, the cloud groups farthest behind it will be moved in
front of its path, so that the pilots will again be traveling within the center
cloud group region. The movement of an entire cloud group should be
achievable by a simple update of the position of its centroid.

The atmosphere will be organized into layers. The ith layer will be at
height z_i above sea level. The atmospheric fading constant of that layer
will be denoted by a_i and the color faded to by c_i. Thus an object within
the ith layer, when viewed through the layer from infinity, will appear to
have color c_i, no matter what its actual color might be.

Fading constants and colors for locations between the planes of the
specified layers will be obtained by linear interpolation. This will be

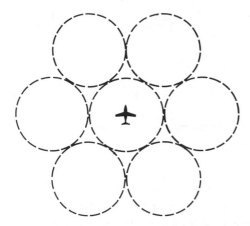

Figure 7.6. The aircraft flying within the center of seven cloud groups.

illustrated with a simple example. Suppose that there is a single atmospheric layer, and the pilot is flying through it along its center plane and viewing an object on the ground (Figure 7.7). The apparent color of the object as viewed by the pilot will be

$$\text{Apparent color} = (\text{Actual color}) * \exp\left[-0.5(a_0 + a_1)d\right] + 0.5(c_0 + c_1)$$
$$* \left\{1 - \exp\left[-0.5(a_0 + a_1)d\right]\right\}$$

where d is the distance between the pilot and the object. The general solution is considerably more complex. There will be a number of atmospheric layers. The pilot may fly anywhere among them. Suppose, for example, that the pilot is in an upper layer viewing an object below. The general solution is then found by first computing the color of the object at the center plane of the layer directly above it, at the point the view line intersects the layer. This value is then treated as the color of a virtual object. The process is repeated by computing the color of this virtual object as it would appear at the center plane of the layer above it. And so on, until the viewpoint is reached.

The atmospheric layer containing the cloud groups should have a high enough fading value to keep newly repositioned groups from appearing to pop into view. This is necessary, because system limitations will prevent large numbers of ellipsoids from being displayed at once. If the pilot enters an individual cloud, the entire visual field should be fogged out.

Storms can be treated as special cloud groups. Storms are generally composed of nimbus clouds, which are darker and of greater vertical extent and higher elevation than cumulus clouds. Storms can be simulated to remain at a fixed location in the atmosphere. Lightning can be simulated by strings of point lights between clouds. The lights within a

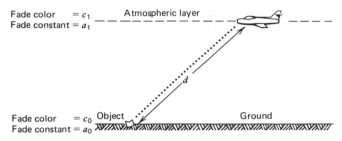

Figure 7.7.   A single atmospheric layer.

string will rapidly flash on and off in sequence at irregular intervals. Strobe lights within the cockpit can be synchronized to the lightning flashes on the display. The brightness of the flashes should be related to the pilot's distance from the simulated lightning bolts.

7.4.   VAPOR AND SMOKE TRAILS

Vapor (or condensation) trails are artificial clouds composed of the water vapor content of a jet engine's exhaust (Figure 7.8). Their visibility is dependent upon local weather conditions. Rockets and missiles emit trails with a higher carbon content, called smoke trails. Often a rocket's trail can be noticed, but not the rocket itself. The following simplifying assumptions can be made:

1.   Jet vapor trails are only visible for jets flying above a specified altitude.
2.   Rocket smoke trails are always visible.

Most vapor and smoke trails can be simulated by strings of long, thin, translucent ellipsoids. They will remain fixed to the tail end of an airborne vehicle, moving with it. Certain rockets are designed to gyrate as they travel. These rockets will have attached helical smoke trails, which will spin with them (Figure 7.9).

7.5.   SHADOWS (FOR A GROUND PLANE/PYRAMID TERRAIN REPRESENTATION SCHEME)

Translucent shadows of fixed size and shape can be attached to 3-D objects. Objects can be rotated before being displayed in the simulated

Figure 7.8. Vapor trail.

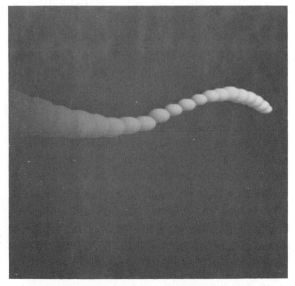

Figure 7.9. Simulated helical smoke trail.

scene, so that their shadows fall away from the sun. This technique is clearly viable only for radially symmetric objects (e.g., some trees, oil tanks, etc.) or for objects whose orientations are immaterial. The low cost of this approach makes it an attractive alternative to designing systems which display no shadows at all.

7.6.   MOVING SURFACE VEHICLES

The paths of moving surface vehicles can be predefined in the data base. Trucks will move along paths over roads, trains over tracks, and boats over rivers. The paths of tanks and other military vehicles may not lie on any visible roadbed.

Paths can be stored as strings of vertices. With a triangular terrain model each vertex should fall on an edge of the triangulation. However, if the terrain representation is hierarchical, there will be problems. A triangular edge at one level of detail will in general not coincide with an edge at the next level of detail. There are two obvious solutions to this problem. One involves displaying a surface vehicle only when its underlying terrain is being displayed at its highest level of detail. A less interesting solution is to use only straight-line paths.

Military simulators may require ground vehicles to take evasive maneuvers when under attack. Certain vertices comprising a path may be labeled as check points. An alternate path will connect one check point to the next. An alternate path may, for example, pass through a forest region. When a vehicle reaches a check point, it will be determined whether it is under attack. If it is, it will speed up and take the alternate path, if not it will continue along the same path at its normal speed.

7.7.   FLARE AND LANDING LIGHT ILLUMINATION

A descending flare does not light up the entire environment the way sunlight does. The sun is nearly at infinity, whereas a flare is within the scene itself. A correct simulation of the illumination of all objects in the environment due to flare light would be extremely difficult. The simulated earth's surface is typically piecewise planar, with 3-D objects placed upon it. The intensity of illumination from a flare should taper off according to the square of the distance between a surface object point and the momentary location of the descending flare. Flare light should cast shadows. The following approach can be used as a simple alternative to mimicking the actual physical effect. The simulation of flare illumination can be achieved on the 2-D projection of the actual 3-D scene. This requires the computation of the intersection point P of the faceted earth's surface and the line segment joining the descending flare to the earth's center. The orientation of the illuminated region in 3-D space can be described by two unit vectors originating at P, one along the line of latitude passing through P, the other along the line of longitude. These vectors define a circle tangent to a spherical earth. The size and brightness of this circle of illumination will be proportional to the height of the flare above P.

This circle, when projected onto the view windows, will be an ellipse, hyperbola, or parabola. The points of intersection of the border of this illuminated region with each raster line must be computed each frame time. For a system that generates imagery one line at a time, the brightness along a scan line can be tapered from the two intersection points toward their center (Figure 7.10).

Landing light illumination can also be approximated by increasing scene brightness within an elliptical region of the 2-D scene. Considering the importance of landing lights to the pilot, it is probably preferable to taper brightness along both axes of an ellipse (Figure 7.11). The failure of

Figure 7.10.   Simulation of flare illumination by a second-order equation along a scanline.

Figure 7.11.   A scene produced by GE's C-130 visual simulator showing the illumination of the runway due to landing lights.

one landing or taxi light can be depicted by changing the size and shape of the illuminated region.

One anomaly that may arise when using the above approach is Mach bands. Mach band patterns can be prevented by performing computations and storing color data to sufficient precision (at least 12-bit color intensity).

7.8.   DYNAMIC SEA STATE

Lewandowski, Hinkle, and Tucker [LEWA80] of Singer/Link describe a technique for depicting a dynamic sea state. The 3-D waves are modeled as small blue planar faceted mounds, with curved-surface shading used for smoothness. They achieve the effect of motion by assigning a special sun vector to the group of faces comprising the ocean surface. This special sun vector is rotated with a circular motion to produce a changing sea state. Different rotation schemes simulate different sea conditions.

Bow and stern wakes around ships are also modeled. One approach is to associate a set of wake faces with a ship. As a moving ship's description is transferred from the data base, one of the wake faces is transferred with it and subsequently displayed. After a fixed number of frames, a pointer

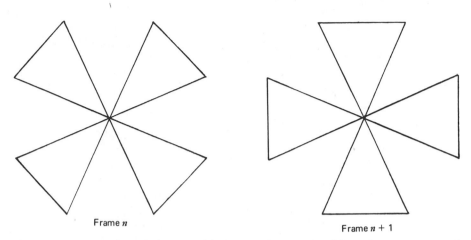

Frame n

Frame $n + 1$

Figure 7.12. Spinning helicopter blades can be simulated by substituting one of the above patterns for the other at the frame rate.

substitutes a second face for the first. The rate at which subsequent faces appear, and their shape and color, yield the desired effect. One problem with this approach is that the effect is lost when the ship is viewed from the front, since the wake faces have no thickness.

Another approach tried was to model wakes in the same manner as ocean waves. Several different patterns, colors, and sun vector angles and motions were tested. It was found that a rapidly changing sun vector produced the desired effect of churning water.

Once sea conditions can be adequately portrayed, it becomes important to simulate the corresponding effects of ship pitch and roll. Lewandowski et al. discuss the many complications involved with this.

7.9. HELICOPTER ROTOR BLADES

Lewandowski et al. [LEWA80] simulate spinning rotor blades by real-time object substitution. Two 45° German crosses are stored, one being a 45° rotated version of the other (Figure 7.12). The two together would form a solid octagon if superimposed. Each of these rotor blades is substituted for the other at the frame rate. The resulting effect is one of flicker or blade rotation.

PART TWO

VLSIC APPROACHES TO COMPUTER IMAGE GENERATION

The next generation of CIG devices will most assuredly be more powerful and of smaller size than those of the current generation. Will this next generation evolve slowly, by piecemeal insertion of VLSI technology, or will a revolution in algorithms and architectures take place? Current indications are that the process will be evolutionary—but revolutions are, of course, difficult to predict.

For new CIG designs to be successful, they must adequately perform three difficult tasks: hidden-surface elimination, antialiasing, and texturing. The solution to hidden-surface elimination must be achieved with reasonable word sizes, even for the long viewing ranges common in flight simulation. Algorithms for hidden-surface elimination must make available scene components in the right order so that antialiasing can be effectively performed. Finally, a variety of textures must be available for placing onto image surfaces. CIG designs that do not include a texture generation capability are uninteresting.

8 THE ROLE OF LSI/VLSI IN COMPUTER IMAGE GENERATION

THOMAS R. HOFFMAN

8.1. INTRODUCTION: THE PROBLEM OF HARDWARE PROLIFERATION

CIG systems, such as those described in Chapter 4, tend to be extremely hardware intensive, and hence very expensive. A combination of the computation rate required to "paint" the picture often enough to avoid flicker and the huge number of geometric calculations necessary to transform a 3-D data base into a 2-D view window scene has forced designers to adopt a pipeline architecture. Although standard components are becoming faster and more logically complex each year, the insatiable desire of CIG users for special features and increased scene detail more than keeps pace. Clever computation schemes are continually being devised to realize these advanced concepts, but each increase in capability inevitably calls for still more hardware. A typical high-performance multichannel CIG system contains more than 150,000 integrated circuits, many of which are already LSI (e.g., memory chips).

Control of this hardware proliferation is one of the most important tasks facing CIG designers. The basic algorithms are, of course, under continual examination in hopes of finding better ways to achieve performance objectives, but now the emerging ability to create integrated circuits of incredible density (hundreds of thousands of transistors per chip) offers a complementary approach. CIG designers must embrace LSI now, and VLSI as it matures, in order to produce systems of acceptable physical size.

173

8.2. WAYS IN WHICH LSI/VLSI CAN BE INTRODUCED

Designers have several strategies available whereby LSI/VLSI can be incorporated into their products. One of these was mentioned in Section 8.1—it is simply ongoing evaluation and adoption, where appropriate, of off-the-shelf LSI/VLSI components. CIG systems tend to be memory intensive. As standard RAM and ROM chips grow from 4K to 16K to 64K to . . . , CIG designers should use chips at or near the crest of the wave. Similarly, large multiplier chips and ALUs of various types are becoming fairly common. Since these too are functions frequently employed in CIG, their adoption is just good engineering practice. It does not seem to be possible to appreciably reduce system size by this strategy alone, but some measure of control can be obtained. Unfortunately CIG does not represent a market sufficiently large to motivate the major semiconductor-device manufacturers to build components specially tailored to it.

What then can be done beyond the use of state-of-the-art standard components? The answer lies in the tremendous effort now being devoted to making semicustom and full-custom integrated circuit design capability available to the typical system designer. Sections 8.3 and 8.4 consider these two possibilities separately.

8.3. SEMICUSTOM COMPONENTS OR "GATE ARRAYS"

A gate array is a silicon die in which some basic cell structure has been replicated many times, in regular fashion. No interconnections between cells (and in some cases, no intraconnections either) have been made. Designers, using logic "macros" provided by the gate array vendor, translate their logic designs into vendor-specified formats. The details of this process vary widely—at least 30 companies offer gate arrays now; it is likely that no two have identical structures and procedures. Figure 8.1 shows a typical product development flow diagram, omitting loops to show that the flow may be recurring at any level as errors are uncovered or design changes are introduced.

Simulation is a vital element of the development process. The conceptual design must be verified before fabrication is begun, or much time and money will be wasted. Then after the verified design is laid out and the cell interconnections are routed, the physical design must be checked to ensure that it obeys design rules and agrees with the original logic in every respect. Only then can silicon processing begin with any reasonable probability of success. Such simulation and double-checking is replacing the more traditional approach of breadboarding, or prototyping, a design.

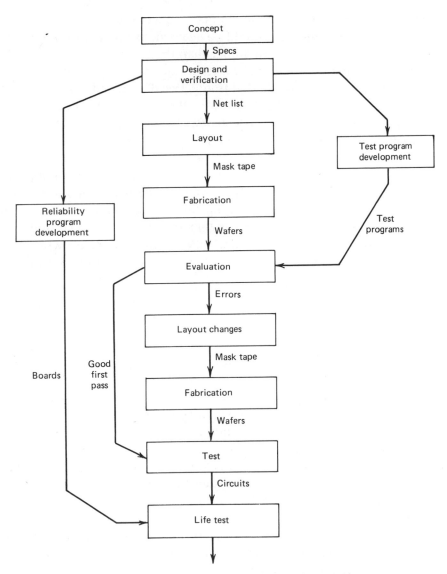

Figure 8.1. Typical product development flow diagram for gate arrays.

The sizes of available gate arrays are increasing rapidly. Common now are 1000-gate arrays; larger sizes are available to the more venturesome designer. A word of caution is in order here, however, since vendors often announce larger arrays than they can handle competently. Unwary customers may find themselves unwilling participants in a research and development effort.

The key to success is the effectiveness of the vendor's CAD tools for the acquisition of circuit descriptions, their simulation, layout, and rule checking. Beyond 1000 gates, manual placement of routing becomes enormously time-consuming and should be avoided, particularly if iterations are necessary, which is the rule rather than the exception.

In summary, the gate-array approach has outstanding potential, but is in such a state of rapid growth, that troublefree design and fabrication are not assured. Despite this R&D flavor to the process, the potential for significant hardware reduction is considerable. One 1000-gate array may replace 40 to 50 integrated circuits of a typical SSI/MSI mix. The savings are worthwhile and should be sought, provided that suitable application areas can be identified. A complete design cycle time of 3 months is not unreasonable, and this will surely shorten as the parties involved gain experience. The overall cost to the customer typically involves a non-recurring charge of from $3000 to $50,000. In addition are the customer's own labor costs, and the cost per production-packaged device, which is a function of volume. Obviously, high volume will allow recovery of development costs, whereas low volume will not.

8.4.   FULL-CUSTOM LSI/VLSI

The design of custom LSI chips has been a standard part of semiconductor device technology for more than a decade. Such designs have been characterized by much manual work, long cycle times (up to 2 years), and high cost. Design iterations were common, since the process is extremely unforgiving. The result has been to limit custom LSI applications to high-volume, stable product applications.

Recent years have witnessed trends at streamlining the custom design process in many ways. Costs and design times have been reduced by a combination of several factors, including:

1.   Development of a methodology whereby system designers can do the integrated circuit design themselves, without the help of semiconductor specialists
2.   Dramatic improvement of CAD tools and ways of teaching their use
3.   Wafer processing by silicon foundry services geared to handle small or large volumes with a short turnaround time.

The design methodology issue (item 1) has achieved widespread acceptance following the publication of the book *Introduction to VLSI Systems* by Mead and Conway [MEAD79]. College students now often graduate with actual custom LSI design experience. Some courses cover the entire process: task selection, chip design, foundry fabrication, and test of the finished product. Short courses are also available for the seasoned design engineer. The notion that only a few specialists can do custom designs is now obsolete.

Again, the ultimate success of the LSI/VLSI design revolution resides in the CAD area. High-level circuit descriptions, verified by advanced simulations, activate automatic placement and routing routines. ERC and DRC runs uncover design errors. A final simulation directly from the layout completes the verification loop.

However, as the design process for LSI custom chips is being brought under control, the design of much larger logic arrays, huge dynamic RAMs, 64-bit floating-point processors, and the like is still a formidable challenge. In the world of VLSI, entire systems are reduced to one or a few chips. It is sometimes said that in this VLSI world, the only standard parts are memories and microprocessors. All else is full-custom, each chip specifically designed for a very particular application. This concept represents a movement away from the usual goal of mass production, since except as previously noted there can be no standard products to fit all applications. One consequence of this trend is that in this area large companies will not have a significant advantage over smaller companies.

Hardware intensive CIG systems will benefit from the streamlining of LSI/VLSI procedures. In the near term, CIG systems will not only use VLSI memory chips, but also computational chips of comparable magnitude, resulting in systems that are more and more VLSI oriented. The realization of major architectural revisions becomes a distinct possibility as more functions are assigned to a single chip.

8.5. THE CONTRIBUTION OF VERY-HIGH-SPEED INTEGRATED CIRCUITRY (VHSIC)

In an attempt to coordinate, at least to some extent, the efforts of the many companies participating in the VLSI explosion, the Department of Defense launched the VHSIC program. Nine industrial contractor teams competed in phase 0 of the program, each defining a set of one or more 1-micron feature-size chips and a brassboard (i.e., a system made up primarily of VHSIC chips). Six of the phase 0 teams were chosen to participate in phase 1, their charge being to build the brassboard defined in phase 0. The final phase 2 effort involves translation of processing techniques to the submicron level, with a result of chips of the 100,000-gate size. Phase 3, running concurrently with phases 0, 1, and 2, provides support for the development of the submicron technology by numerous contractors, including but not limited to the phase 1 winners.

VHSIC technology—chips and brassboards—will be made available to interested defense contractors, whether or not they are VHSIC contractors. The programmable nature of many of the VHSIC chips will make them applicable to systems other than those for which they were originally intended. CIG is a prime candidate for their adaptation. None of the major CIG designers of Chapter 4 is a phase 1 VHSIC contractor, but all hope to benefit from the VHSIC program. Some are already investing private funds to be ready to capitalize on VHSIC developments.

8.6.   SUMMARY AND SOME RECENT VLSI ACCOMPLISHMENTS

Solid-state circuits inexorably continue to benefit from the spread of VLSI technology, operating at higher and higher speeds while at the same time achieving higher and higher densities. A brief list of some of the state-of-the-art devices that were reported upon at the February 1982 International Solid-State Circuits Conference follows:

288K dynamic RAM, using 2-μm NMOS process

6000-gate logic arrays, with 2-μm CMOS process

subnanosecond 2500-gate master slice ECL array

30,000-transistor bipolar microprocessor containing 4708 logic gates, 14 PLAs, and a 13K-bit ROM

64-bit floating-point processor capable of performing 1 million scalar operations per second (separate add, multiply, and divide chips)

completely integrated 32-bit processor system using only 6 VLSI chip types, with 1-μm NMOS process.

The message to CIG designers is clear. Gate arrays are already here, improved custom LSI/VLSI design techniques are developing rapidly, and the VHSIC program will soon provide specific devices to be considered for adaptation as well as advancing the general state of the art. Judicious combination of these approaches, along with continued algorithm evaluation, will lead to CIG systems that exhibit both improved performance and substantial hardware reduction.

9 VLSIC ARCHITECTURES FOR IMAGE GENERATION

RICHARD WEINBERG

9.1. INTRODUCTION

During the 1980s flight simulation visual systems will be strongly influenced by the rapid pace of development of new microelectronic components. Visual systems will take advantage of standard, semicustom, and custom integrated circuits ranging from SSI (small-scale integrated circuits) to VLSI (very-large-scale integrated circuits). The use of the different components will be dictated as strongly by economics as by technology.

Standard components are readily available general-purpose integrated circuits. Standard components span the entire range of integrated circuit complexity from small to medium, large, and very large scale integration, with functions ranging from individual gates to microprocessors. These components are available in several common logic families, including CMOS, TTL, and ECL. Standard microelectronic components have been the mainstay of visual system construction. The development of progressively more powerful general-purpose microprocessors will provide new tools for the construction of new visual systems. The use of these existing, inexpensive, well-documented components leads to the simplest, if not always the most elegant or desirable design.

Semicustom integrated circuits offer the system designer a middle ground between standard and custom integrated circuits. The system designer specifies the logic or the functions to be provided by the semicustom integrated circuits. The supplier of the semicustom integrated circuits then builds them to these specifications as a final step in the manufacturing process. The semicustom approach provides faster system development than fully custom chips for several reasons. First, the circuits being designed using this method are usually less complex than those requiring full customization. Second, the semicustom chip supplier can stockpile semicompleted chips and perform the final manufacturing steps upon demand. Finally, it is simpler to develop tools for semicustom chips than for custom chips, since the initial geometry of semicustom chips is fixed beforehand. Semicustom chips include gate arrays.

Custom integrated circuits provide the designer the greatest flexibility, but at the greatest cost. With full-custom design, system designers can tailor the integrated circuits exactly to their needs. The full architecture of the circuit is under the designer's control, including the registers, arithmetic units, data paths, control, timing, pin layout, and packaging. However, this flexibility is purchased at the cost of a more complex development, simulation, and testing cycle. To justify the time and expense required for custom design, there must be a significant demand for the components. Only when neither standard components nor semicustom components provide the necessary speed, size, functionality, cost, or performance should fully custom components be designed.

Manufacturers should use custom or semicustom integrated circuits in flight simulation for one of two reasons. First, they may want to replace some of the logic functions in their current systems with fewer components for cost or size reduction and reliability enhancement. In this case, no new functionality is gained, but there may be an economic benefit. Second, manufacturers may utilize custom or semicustom integrated circuits in new designs which are only possible or practical with VLSI. The motivation in this case is to build systems which are less expensive, more reliable, more compact, and provide better performance.

9.2. PARALLEL AND PIPELINE PROCESSING ARCHITECTURES

Implementing a real-time high-complexity image synthesis system requires the use of a special-purpose architecture to achieve the fast data rates needed to produce images. Parallel and pipeline architectures attempt to meet the speed demand by partitioning the image generation problem among many processors, each operating concurrently. Three basic approaches can be taken, or combined, in partitioning the image generation problem. These three approaches are (1) large-scale pipelined systems, (2) partitioning the image space, and (3) partitioning the object space.

9.3.   LARGE-SCALE PIPELINE ARCHITECTURES

Most recent systems have used a pipeline approach which processes each frame of data in several stages, so that at any time, several successive frames are in different stages of partial completion and pass through the pipeline to the final video output.

In these real-time graphics systems, the philosophy has been to use specialized high-performance processors, each capable of performing a partial transformation on a full frame's worth of data in a frame's time. Each of these processors is specialized for its particular task (e.g., object transformation, hidden surface removal, or pixel shading) and is relatively inflexible; extending a polygon machine to a bicubic patch machine is not feasible.

Because the design of a graphics system is quite complex, large systems may contain hundreds of printed circuit boards with MSI, LSI, and VLSI circuits, several cooperating processors, and many pipeline stages. Furthermore, the number of different board types within a given system is quite large. This complexity is illustrated in the CT-3 system built by Evans and Sutherland.

CT-3 is a 2-channel image synthesizer for real-time Space Shuttle flight simulation. The unit contains some 800 cards with over 100 different card types. This complexity leads us to search for alternate, simpler designs.

9.4.   PARTITIONING THE IMAGE SPACE WITH PROCESSORS

Parallel processing may be used in image synthesis by partitioning the image space among a number of processors. Each of these processors is responsible for a region of the image or screen. This type of partitioning breaks up the processing among the processors so that each of them operates concurrently, with a processing task less demanding than computing the entire image. The main considerations are (1) how to partition the screen, (2) how to distribute tasks to the processors, and, once the image has been generated by the processors, (3) how to unite it from the separate processors to generate a video image.

The number of assignments grows rapidly with the size of the image, and clearly some assignments are better than others for hidden-surface calculations. A central question is, how should the pixels be assigned to the processors?

Those devices, which partition the image space, can be classified by the following criteria:

1. Assignment of pixels to processors
   a. Fixed
   b. Variable
2. Shape and size of processor's pixel region
   a. Fixed
   b. Variable
3. Connectivity of processor's pixel region
   a. Contiguous
   b. Noncontiguous

Note that this classification scheme deals only with the problem of mappings between processors and pixels.

9.4.1.   Assignment of Processors to Pixels

9.4.1.1.   Fixed Assignment Systems

This family ranges from the most common case of one very fast processor (probably a pipelined system) assigned to compute an entire $n \times m$ pixel image to the ultimate processing scheme with one processor per pixel. In between this range is a system with one processor for the odd and one processor for the even lines, for every jth line, and so on. The screen could also be partitioned into rectangles or squares or noncontiguous regions. An example of this class is the pixel processors for Clark's geometry engine [CLAR80, CLAR82].

9.4.1.2.   Variable Assignment Systems

Kaplan [KAPL79] has reported on the simulation of a system which has free processors selected from a pool to perform calculations as needed. With such a scheme, a scheduling algorithm is required to assign tasks to processors. However, tasks may be assigned to processors using some criteria for optimizing system utilization.

9.4.2. Shape and Size of Pixel Regions

9.4.2.1. Fixed Size and Shape

An example of a system with a fixed size and shape is a device having a large number of processors, each of which can process a line of the screen. When the processing of a line is complete, the processor is free to act upon another line, but the assignment of processors to lines in the image may vary from frame to frame.

9.4.2.2. Variable Size and Shape

In order to keep the processors busy, the assignment of processors to pixels could be dynamic. The processors concentrate where the hardest problems are, similar to the way in which the Warnock algorithm subdivides the screen until all of the visible surface questions are easy to solve. With this type of subdivision, the final regions will differ in size. If we assign processors in some manner to these regions, then they will have different amounts of information to report, since their domain is of variable size. Such an architecture would enjoy the advantage of keeping a minimum number of processors busy in regions that have few surfaces or only simple decisions. A processor's pixel region could also assume the size and shape of the object currently assigned to it.

9.4.3. Connectivity of Pixel Regions

9.4.3.1. Contiguous Pixel Regions

Finally, we note the distinction between contiguous and noncontiguous processors. A processor is contiguous if all of the pixels in its domain are connected, that is, for each processor p there is a path completely contained in p's pixels, from every pixel p_1 to every pixel p_2 in p. If this is not the case for each of the processors, then the system is noncontiguous. All existing CIG systems use contiguous mappings.

9.4.3.2. Noncontiguous Pixel Regions

A noncontiguous processor described by Fuchs [FUCH79a] uses interleaved timing to take advantage of the noncontiguous (but regular) ordering of the pixels. In this system the screen is divided among a collection of processors. Each processor has a section of image memory (r, g, b) along with a z buffer for each pixel in its domain, and each processor is responsible for the corresponding region of the raster screen.

Polygons are broadcast to the pixel processors in arbitrary order. Whenever a polygon is broadcast and may be visible at a given pixel, the pixel's z-buffer location is checked to determine whether the new polygon is closer to the viewer than the current closest polygon. If the new polygon is closer, the new color value replaces the old value, and the new z distance replaces the old z distance. This process continues until all polygons have been broadcast. The image buffer then contains the desired image, which is scanned out and converted to video.

The z-buffer algorithm is not well suited to solving aliasing problems since it is basically a point sampling method. Since the polygons may arrive in any order, the interactions within the pixel which cause aliasing problems cannot be properly examined. To perform antialiasing properly, the entire list of visible or partially visible objects in each pixel's domain must be stored. Since each processor's pixels are scattered throughout the screen, and may have an entirely different list of partially visible objects, each pixel would need an (extensive) area for additional storage.

This problem arises since the polygons are not broadcast to the processors in any particular order. The first and the last polygons typically hit most of the processors. The solution is either to retain the entire list for the entire frame calculation period or to perform incremental subpixel visible surface determinations. Alternately, we may try to increase the resolution of the system and then average the colors at subpixel resolution to get final colors, which would increase the memory and speed requirements in proportion to the square of the increase in resolution.

Parke [PARK80] has simulated a distributed z-buffer system also, and has examined various ways of distributing the objects to the processors. However, the same problems with antialiasing remain.

Fuchs [FUCH81] presents another architecture based on VLSI for an intelligent frame buffer with parallel processing at the pixel level.

9.5. PARTITIONING THE OBJECT SPACE WITH PROCESSORS

The process of image synthesis may also be broken down by partitioning the object space: assigning objects to different concurrently operating processors. This type of organization allows (1) many processors to split the total task of converting objects to images, (2) multiple types of objects to coexist in the system, each object residing in a specialized processor, and

(3) object-capacity increases to be incremental by adding more processors. The problems encountered are in the allocation of the objects to the processors and the recombining of the outputs of the many processors into the final image.

Although parallel processing remains a current research topic, even the earliest real-time flight simulation systems used a high degree of parallelism. The General Electric system at NASA, for example, the first real-time flight simulation graphics system, had a processor for each edge in the environment [SCHU69]. This type of system utilizes object space partitioning, since objects reside in different processors, whose outputs are recombined. These processors then generate the final image in real time using an algorithm developed by Schumacker.

Cohen [COHE80] has proposed a device based on custom integrated circuits which implement a pixel by pixel in-or-out decision processor. Processors are connected serially. Each processor receives an object to scan convert. A processor either passes on the pixel data (color plus depth) it receives, or replaces it to achieve hidden surface removal if its own object is closer. Again, antialiasing is a problem since pixel coverage is not available at the appropriate time, and only one object can be selected as the visible object at each pixel. Increased resolution would help, but at the expense of speed.

This type of serially connected structure provides the basis for [WEIN81], a parallel processing architecture which includes antialiasing. The proposed VLSI design combines object and image space partitioning, and achieves antialiasing by determining visible surfaces at subpixel resolution and filtering the results [WEIN82].

9.6. CONCLUSIONS

In the future we should expect visual systems for flight simulation to exploit various types of high-performance integrated circuits. A wide variety of architectures remain to be explored for use in this computationally demanding application of electronic technology. Special-purpose integrated circuits may be developed in the future, which will aid in the development of these devices. Some of the functions which could be performed by these circuits include geometric transformations, clipping, frame buffer control, run-length decoding, video control, hidden-surface removal, texturing and antialiasing. Economics will determine when these functions will be implemented as special-purpose integrated circuits, and the ingenuity of the system designer will determine how they are best used for image generation.

PART THREE

TRAINING

"Those wishing to take up aviation training either as a recreation or a profession find many drawbacks at the commencement of their undertaking, but one of the most formidable, especially to those not blessed with a long purse, is the risk of smashing the machine while endeavoring to learn to control and fly it.

. . . The invention, therefore, of a device which will enable the novice to obtain a clear conception of the workings of the control of an aeroplane, and of the conditions existent in the air, without any risk personally or otherwise, is to be welcomed without a doubt.

. . . Now there is a tendency to design such an apparatus merely for the purpose of balance and without any real resemblance to an actual aeroplane, while the very balance is so exaggerated that the pupil is placed under conditions that are in no way so arduous in free flight."

Flight International
December 10, 1910,

Almost three quarters of a century has passed since these comments were made about the earliest attempts at aircraft simulation. Yet today, there

This introduction is taken from a pamphlet distributed by the Naval Training Equipment Center. The remaining chapters are from the *Defense Management Journal*, Fourth Quarter, 1980, and are used by permission.

are still many questions being asked about the requirements for simulator design and the correspondence between the training device and the airplane it simulates. The articles in this section, taken from a special issue of the *Defense Management Journal*, address these questions.

10 AN OVERVIEW OF MILITARY TRAINING-SYSTEM DEVELOPMENT

ALLEN COLLIER

Each branch of the armed services has its own organization for the acquisition of training equipment. The Naval Training Equipment Center at Orlando, Florida, is the principal procurer for the Navy and Marine Corps. The center is under the Chief of Naval Education and Training, located in Pensacola, Florida. The Army's procurer, the Project Manager for Training Devices (PM TRADE), is also located at the Orlando facility and reports to the Deputy Commanding General for Materiel Development, U.S. Army Materiel Development and Readiness Command. Managing the major portion of the Air Force's acquisition of simulators is the Deputy for Simulators, who reports to the Aeronautical Systems Division of the Air Force Systems Command, Wright-Patterson Air Force Base, Ohio.

Because the Naval Training Equipment Center is chartered to improve the effectiveness of training and training materiel support programs through research and development, test and evaluation, procurement, and logistics support, its mission is more broadly based than that of its counterparts. Not surprisingly, the other services and the Coast Guard frequently utilize its technical expertise and capabilities.

To ensure that configuration changes to a parent system do not render the training equipment obsolete, the center maintains an active modernization and modification program. The center's logistics engineers and

This chapter is an abridged version of an article originally published in the *Defense Management Journal*.

provisioning specialists work closely with both users and manufacturers to ensure the continued availability of spare and replacement parts.

Requirements for Army training equipment, which are established by the U.S. Army Training and Doctrine Command, come to PM TRADE from the U.S. Army Training Support Center at Fort Eustis, Virginia. In managing the various programs, PM TRADE assigns responsibility for individual projects to subordinate project managers, who are supported by the PM TRADE and by appropriate departments in the Naval Training Equipment Center. The relationship between PM TRADE and the Naval Training Equipment Center is an ongoing example of interservice cooperation, one that dates back to 1950 with the signing of an agreement between the Army and the Navy. This pact called for the Army to establish a cadre and to use their expertise at what was then the Navy Special Devices Center in Port Washington, New York.

For the Air Force, training requirements are expressed in a Statement of Operational Need by the using command. The Air Force Systems Command then evaluates these training requirements and offers suitable options. If Headquarters Air Force validates and authorizes funding for the Statement of Operational Need, approval to purchase the requisite equipment is transmitted to the Air Force Systems Command as part of a program management directive. This directive provides general guidance and identifies program resources. The Air Force Systems Command then selects the appropriate field command to manage the resulting program.

Since May 1973, the Deputy for Simulators has been managing the engineering development, testing, and deployment of all new Air Force aircrew training simulators. In July 1978, the Deputy for Simulators also assumed responsibility for new maintenance training simulators.

Headquarters Air Force Logistics Command and the Odgen Air Logistics Center help ensure that simulators are supportable for the life of their parent system. Once a simulator is delivered to the operating command, responsibility for its maintenance, including configuration control, modification planning, and spare parts, belongs to the system manager at Odgen Air Logistics Center.

11 REAPING THE BENEFITS OF FLIGHT SIMULATION

JESSE ORLANSKY AND JOSEPH STRING

Flight training is one of the more glamorous as well as expensive types of training conducted by the Department of Defense. In fiscal year 1980 it cost $1.8 billion to train some 5800 students who entered undergraduate pilot training. Postgraduate flight training is conducted in operational commands and is excluded from these data. Large costs are also expended to train pilots to fly combat aircraft and to become proficient in the tactics required for their most effective use. While it is difficult to establish the exact costs, estimates on the order of $750,000 to $1,000,000 to train a single combat pilot are probably realistic.

Pilots prefer to train in aircraft rather than in flight simulators for two obvious reasons:

1. Pilots would rather fly than sit in a box on the ground.
2. Many of the older simulators are poor training devices because of inadequate handling qualities. (The military services did not do enough to improve flight simulators during the 1960s.)

But this latter situation changed quickly after the oil embargo of 1973 when it became apparent that fuel would be more costly, less available, and hence more of a constraint on training. Early in 1974, Deputy Secretary of Defense W. P. Clements told Congress that the Department of Defense would try to reduce total flying hours. Increased funds were provided to procure new flight simulators and additional funds were pro-

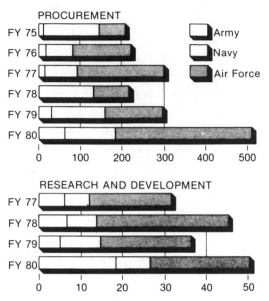

Figure 11.1. Funding for flight simulators (millions of dollars).

vided for research and development to improve existing simulators (Figure 11.1).

A flight simulator is neither an aircraft nor a substitute for flying an aircraft. Even a flight simulator that has very high fidelity is still a training device. Nonetheless, flight simulators offer many advantages: they permit close observation of pilot performance, they provide immediate feedback of information, and they permit a pilot to experience malfunctions and flight conditions rarely encountered in actual flight. Moreover, they are very convenient to use, have greater availability than aircraft, and can save lives.

But flight simulators also have significant limitations in their dynamic responses due to incomplete flight data with which to specify their performance close to the ground. Even with good platform motion, they are still bolted to the ground, and their visual systems leave room for improvement. Simulators also are expensive to buy and operate.

It seems clear that modern flight simulators should have some role in training military pilots. In practical terms, this means that data on the cost and effectiveness of flight simulators and aircraft must be evaluated. Excluded from consideration in this analysis is the use of flight simulators for purposes other than training, such as for the development of aircraft or of tactics for combat. Also excluded from consideration is the value of simulators for training civilian or commercial pilots.

We start by considering how much flight simulators and aircraft cost to operate. For this purpose we consider only variable operating costs, which by definition include the costs of fuel, oil and lubricants, base maintenance materials, and the portion of depot maintenance which varies with flying hours and replenishment spares. Variable operating costs do not include the costs of crew and student salaries or of amortizing the procurement of simulators.

Data on the cost per hour of operating 33 aircraft and simulators are shown in Figure 11.2. The data are based on actual utilization of these aircraft and simulators for fiscal years 1975 and 1976.

Most cost ratios between operating simulators and aircraft vary about 5 to 20 percent. The median value is about 12 percent. On the basis of operating costs alone, it is clear that it costs less to operate a flight simulator than a comparable aircraft. However, this cost advantage says nothing about training effectiveness.

There are many ways to evaluate the effectiveness of flight simulators for use in military training. A favorite one is to have experienced pilots judge whether a simulator flies about the same as a comparable aircraft. This is test by "fidelity of simulation." Pilots can be quite vocal about the fidelity of a simulator, but this type of evaluation must be handled as subjective data.

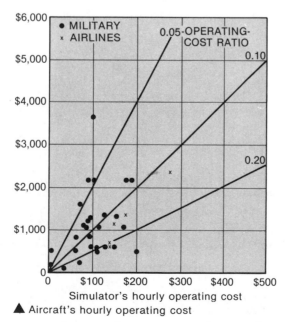

Figure 11.2.   The cost of operating simulators and aircraft.

Since we were concerned with the use of flight simulators for flight training, we were particularly interested in whether skills learned in a simulator carry over to an airplane. That is called "transfer of training" and is measured in terms of transfer effectiveness ratios. Between 1939 and 1977 there were 33 studies published that provide this type of information.

These studies were performed in simulators that vary widely with respect to types of aircraft and their visual and motion systems. About half of the studies were performed after 1970, when modern simulators became available. The studies also vary with respect to the level of pilot experience and the types of flying tasks that were examined.

Taken as a group, these studies show that pilots trained in simulators perform in aircraft as well as those trained only in aircraft, at least as measured by the ratings of instructor pilots. This finding applies to such tasks as cockpit checkout, flight procedures, instrument flying, and takeoff and landing; a few recent studies extend these findings to acrobatic maneuvers and air-to-ground gunnery.

The studies also indicate that simulator training seems to save flight time. However, the results of these studies were not reported in a common format that would permit a generalization on how much flight time can be saved by simulators. Still, enough information was available from 22 of the studies to compute the transfer effectiveness ratios [ROSC71] shown in Figure 11.3. These ratios include studies of instrument training, transi-

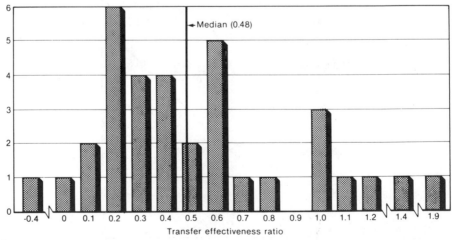

Figure 11.3. Transfer effectiveness ratios (34) derived from 22 studies (1967–1977) show that pilots trained in simulators use less flight time than pilots trained only in aircraft.

tion training, flight procedures, simulators with or without motion, and so forth. The ratios vary from −0.4 to 1.9, with a median value of 0.48.

What these ratios tell us is that pilots trained in simulators use less flight time than those trained only in aircraft. The median amount of flight time saved was about half (0.48) of the time spent in the simulator. There is one negative value (−0.4), which indicates that pilots trained in a simulator in that study used more aircraft time than those trained only in aircraft. Although the information is insufficient to explain this case of "negative transfer," informal inquiry suggests that this result is probably due to use of an inadequate simulator. It is helpful to understand that not all uses of simulators necessarily save training time.

There are seven cases where the transfer effectiveness ratio is 1 or more. These cases indicate that more than 1 hour of flight time was saved for every hour spent in the simulator. This may be due to the fact that one can practice a task more often in 1 hour in a simulator than in an aircraft; for example, in a simulator one does not have to go around the traffic pattern to attempt another landing, nor does one have to take time to set up a flight condition, since this can be done instantly by the computer. However, the high positive ratios and the one negative ratio are extreme values, with the middle 50 percent of all values falling between 0.25 and 0.75.

The ratios were divided into three groups based on the experience levels of the pilots and the different types of training associated with each level, as follows:

1. Highly experienced (advanced pilots)
2. Graduate (pilots who have already earned their wings)
3. Undergraduate (student pilots who have not yet earned their wings)

The results (Figure 11.4) show that undergraduate pilots save more aircraft time as a result of using simulators than do more advanced pilots. It costs more per hour to fly an advanced aircraft than one used by undergraduate pilots, but that is not considered here.

In a recent study, transfer effectiveness ratios were determined for 24 different maneuvers when the CH-47 helicopter flight simulator was used for transition training [HOLM79]. The findings show that transfer effectiveness ratios varied from a high of 2.8 for a four-wheel taxi maneuver to 0.0 for a maneuver known as a pinnacle approach. Clearly this simulator should *not* be used for training on some maneuvers. There is also a strong

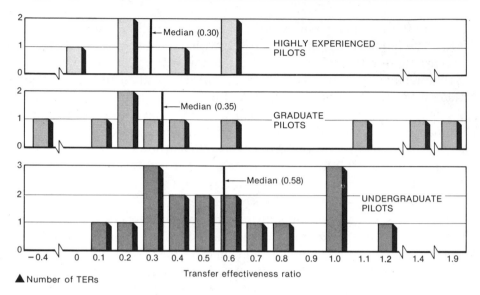

Figure 11.4. Undergraduate pilots save more aircraft time by using simulators than do more advanced pilots.

suggestion that this simulator is not very successful in training on tasks that depend significantly on visual simulation of maneuvers close to the ground.

On the whole, these studies warrant the following conclusions.

Flight Simulators Save Aircraft Time. All but one of the 22 studies show that the use of flight simulators saves aircraft time. Pilots trained on specific tasks in simulators need less time to perform these tasks in aircraft than do pilots trained only in aircraft.

Simulators Are Effective under Many Different Conditions. Simulators have been shown to be effective for training undergraduate and graduate pilots, for training on many different types of aircraft, and for training on such different tasks as landing, instrument flight, and flight familiarization. This finding also applies to the effectiveness of simulators with a variety of performance capabilities, that is, with or without vision and with or without motion.

Effectiveness Varies Widely. There is a wide range in the reported degree of effectiveness. Since most studies do not use common measures, it is difficult to understand the reasons for the wide range in the effectiveness of different types of simulators or of their use for training on different tasks.

Effectiveness Does Not Imply Cost Effectiveness.   The fact that flight simulators are effective for training does not necessarily imply that they are worth their cost.

To estimate the cost effectiveness of flight simulators for training, one needs data in the same study on both the cost and the effectiveness of simulators and of aircraft for training pilots on particular maneuvers or tasks. There are only a few cases where such data have been collected.

A study by Povenmire and Roscoe [POVE73] shows exactly how a cost effectiveness analysis of training should be conducted. Student pilots were given either 0.3, 7, or 11 hours of training on a Link GAT-1 simulator before being trained in an airplane (a Piper Cherokee). Figure 11.5 shows the number of hours needed by each group to pass the final flight check and the number of aircraft hours saved by the simulator when compared to pilots trained only in the airplane. To the best of our knowledge, this is the only study performed so far in which the amount of time spent in a simulator was varied systematically.

On the GAT-1 simulator, both the cumulative transfer effectiveness ratio and the incremental ratio were reduced as the amount of time in the

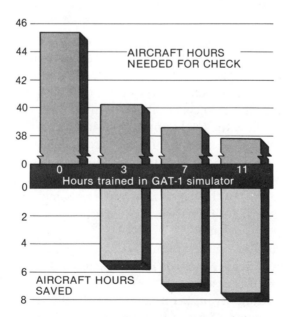

Figure 11.5.   The effect of simulator training on the time needed to pass the final flight check on a Piper Cherokee.

simulator increased. This is an important finding because it permits one to determine when a maximum cost-effective use of the simulator has been reached. A useful criterion is the trade-off between the relative costs of operating the simulator and the aircraft. In this case the simulator-to-aircraft operating cost ratio is $16 to $22 per hour, or 0.73. Therefore training in the simulator is cost-effective until the incremental ratio drops below the simulator-to-aircraft operating cost ratio. This occurs at about 4 hours in the GAT-1 for training student pilots to pass the final flight check for a private pilot's license.

The Piper Cherokee is a simple airplane and at $22 per hour is very inexpensive to operate. The operating costs of most military aircraft range from $200 to $2000 per hour. As reported earlier, most simulator-to-aircraft operating cost ratios range between 0.05 and 0.20. If those ratios applied to the present data, it would have been economical to use the simulator for longer periods, perhaps even as long as 20 hours.

The Coast Guard operates two helicopters, the HH-52A and the HH-3F [ISLE74]. In 1974 it introduced a simulator called the variable cockpit training system. This simulator has two cockpits, can simulate either or both helicopters, and has a motion base with 6 degrees of freedom but no visual system. The procurement cost was $3.1 million. The operating cost per hour of the simulator, $59 in 1974 dollars, is much less than the $504 and $815 for the HH-52A and HH-3F, respectively.

The Coast Guard also introduced a new training syllabus for its new simulator. Figure 11.6 shows the number of aircraft and simulator hours per pilot required to complete various types of training before and after introduction of the simulator. In every case, aircraft hours per pilot were reduced. Whereas the total cost of flight training used to be more than $3 million per year, now the total annual cost, including the additional cost of using the simulator, is $1.6 million, a realized benefit of over $1.4 million. Reduced flight time accounts for the overall savings.

There is another estimated benefit as well. Since the simulator is now used in preparation for the check ride and emergency procedure tests in proficiency training, additional costs of about $1.1 million per year were also avoided.

Thus, the procurement cost of the variable cockpit training system can be amortized in either 2.1 years or 1.2 years, depending on which benefits are used to make this assessment.

In 1977 Browning, Ryan, Scott, and Smode [BROW77] compared the cost and effectiveness of two programs for transition training of Navy pilots on the P-3C, a four-engine, turboprop aircraft used in antisubmarine

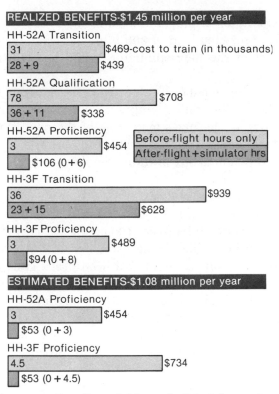

REALIZED BENEFITS-$1.45 million per year

HH-52A Transition
- 31 | $469-cost to train (in thousands)
- 28 + 9 | $439

HH-52A Qualification
- 78 | $708
- 36 + 11 | $338

HH-52A Proficiency
- 3 | $454 | Before-flight hours only
- | $106 (0 + 6) | After-flight + simulator hrs

HH-3F Transition
- 36 | $939
- 23 + 15 | $628

HH-3F Proficiency
- 3 | $489
- | $94 (0 + 8)

ESTIMATED BENEFITS-$1.08 million per year

HH-52A Proficiency
- 3 | $454
- | $53 (0 + 3)

HH-3F Proficiency
- 4.5 | $734
- | $53 (0 + 4.5)

Figure 11.6. The Coast Guard's variable cockpit training system, introduced in 1974 at a cost of $3.1 million, can be amortized in 2.1 years or less.

warfare. These programs involved the use of either an old simulator (2F69D) or a new one (2F87F). Both simulators provided individual and crew training for the pilot, copilot, and flight engineer.

All pilots were newly designated first-tour naval aviators who possessed standard instrument cards. All had completed undergraduate training on the S-2, a two-engine, propeller-driven aircraft. Hours given to training in simulators prior to flight were 22 in the old program, 40 in the new one. After training in the simulator, performance was measured in the aircraft on 20 of the 45 tasks specified in the familiarization and instrument phase of transition training. The critical data were the hours required by each group to perform these tasks proficiently in the aircraft, as judged acceptable by the instructor pilots. The control group required 15 hours per pilot and the experimental group required 9. There was no difference between the groups, in flight proficiency. These findings are also supported by more recent work [BROW78].

The new P-3C simulator costs $4.2 million. Compared to the control program, the experimental program is estimated to save $2.5 million per year, assuming a projected load of 200 pilots per year. On this basis, the procurement cost of the new simulator would be amortized within 2 years.

An analysis of investment costs also favors the new program. Based on required flight hours, the control program would need 7 aircraft, the new one only 4.2 aircraft. The investment cost of the new program is $63.2 million, compared to $98.7 million for the old one. The 10-year life-cycle cost of the new program is $81 million compared to $125 million for the old one.

One airline provided an analysis of 1976 training costs for the use of simulators and aircraft (Figure 11.7). For training it used its simulators for 26,000 hours and its aircraft for over 1100 hours. The cost of these training hours was $6.8 million. The airline estimated that it would have cost about $32.1 million if only aircraft had been used. Thus the airline estimated that its annual training costs were about 21 percent of what they would have been if it had to depend only on aircraft.

The flight simulators used by this airline cost $17.5 million. The airline estimates that it saves $25 million per year using such simulators, thus permitting the airline to amortize the simulator procurement cost in less than 9 months.

It is no surprise to find that it costs less to operate flight simulators than it does to operate aircraft. Most simulator-to-aircraft operating cost ratios are in the range of 0.05 to 0.20. The use of flight simulators reduces aircraft flight time. The range of these values, expressed as transfer effec-

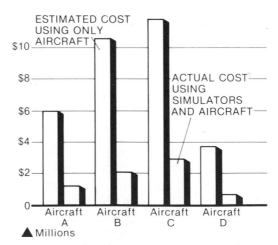

Figure 11.7.   One airline's comparison of annual training costs.

tiveness ratios, varies from close to zero to well over 1, with a median at about 0.50. Thus there is a clear finding that flight simulators can be cost-effective for training, provided that careful attention is given to the tasks and maneuvers for which they are used, and that they are not used beyond the point of marginal utility for these maneuvers. A few studies of cost effectiveness have been conducted, and they indicate that the cost of procuring flight simulators can be amortized in about 2 years.

Several recent developments could significantly affect the cost effectiveness of flight simulators. The first concerns the need for platform motion in flight simulators. A 6-degree-of-freedom synergistic motion platform can cost up to $600,000. A number of studies since 1974 have shown that there is no difference in performance in aircraft between pilots trained in simulators with motion and pilots trained without motion. Although more research remains to be done, it appears that modern flight simulators for center-thrust aircraft, with good visual systems, do not need platform motion. Recent procurements of F-16 and A-10 simulators by the Air Force do not include platform motion. It is still not known whether platform motion is needed in simulators for wide-bodied aircraft. Commercial airlines continue to procure motion bases for their new flight simulators, probably to ensure that the pilots will accept such training.

Over the last 15 years, concern for improving the fidelity of flight simulators led to the improvement of platform motion. It, of course, is true that pilots perform better in simulators with motion than in simulators without motion. Until Koonce's study in 1974, no one had thought to ask whether platform motion in simulators contributes anything to performance in aircraft [KOON79]. The answer so far seems to be that it does not contribute much.

Visual systems for flight simulators are very impressive devices. So is their cost, which ranges from $6 million to $8 million or more per copy. New computer-generated visual systems now can present scenes needed for training in the areas of aerial refueling, air-to-air combat, and nap-of-the-earth flying. The real question, however, concerns the degree of realism required to make visual displays useful for such types of training. Very little data are now available to help us specify the needed visual requirements.

The cost of fuel for aircraft continues to rise. Secretary of Defense Harold Brown made a supplemental request of $3.8 billion for aircraft fuel because of increases in cost beyond that shown in the initial budget for fiscal year 1980. Certainly such cost increases can only make the cost effectiveness relationship more favorable for flight simulators.

It is quite likely that flight simulators will be found to be cost-effective.

As a result, there may be pressure to reduce flying hours. But flight simulators, however useful they may be, are not a substitute for training in aircraft. Military training must proceed from simulators to aircraft, and there must be a minimum amount of actual flight time below which the services cannot go. This is necessary for the maintenance of combat skills and the exercise of maintenance-and-support and command-and-control systems. Clearly, more attention will have to be given to determining what the minimum number of flying hours should be for ensuring military readiness, regardless of the benefits derived from sophisticated flight simulators.

12 THE ARMY'S COUNTERATTACK ON TRAINING COSTS

JEROME A. POGORZELSKI

12.1. INTRODUCTION

In 1974 the Army chartered a Project Manager, Training Devices, for the purpose of managing development and acquisition of training services. Currently PM TRADE manages some 70 training devices in various stages of development. A small sampling of these projects will provide insight into the types of training devices under consideration and the level of technology being applied in this effort.

12.2. ENGAGEMENT SIMULATION

Engagement simulation has received significant attention in recent years. The aim is to enable soldiers to learn and practice those skills essential to survival and achievement of combat victory. These skills range from the individual rifleman protecting himself while inflicting casualties on the enemy to the battalion commander maneuvering forces to counter an enemy attack. Two devices designed for this are the multiple integrated laser engagement system (MILES) and the Army training battle simulation system (ARTBASS).

Providing the smoke and noise of combat, MILES realistically indicates casualties in real time. A variety of MILES transmitters shoot eye-safe gallium arsenide laser beams in place of bullets from each of the direct-fire weapons found in combined-arms maneuver units. By coded pulses of the laser beam, each weapon provides a unique signature which, when detected by silicon photocells located on the target and interpreted by on-board electronics, determines the capability of the firing weapon to inflict damage to the target. Transmitter and detector characteristics are designed to replicate the range characteristics of the respective weapon systems to produce a realistic miss, hit, or kill determination.

Detectors are both worn by men and mounted on vehicles; when activated by a laser, an alarm sounds. A short tone indicates a near miss, which allows for the simulation of the suppression effect of area-fire weapons. A continuous tone signifies a kill. To silence the annoying alarm, the soldier must remove a special key from the firing mechanism. This deactivates the mechanism and decommissions the vehicle or individual. The target is, in effect, a casualty. Since the laser can only be activated by the sound of a blank round or other weapons-signature device firing, realism is enhanced.

Several MILES direct-fire components are at present in production. Development is also underway to expand the system to include air–ground engagements. Simulation of indirect-fire weapons, mines, and other weaponry is envisioned for the near future.

ARTBASS, another form of engagement simulation, is used in training maneuver battalion commanders and their staff in the control and coordination of combined-arms operations. It allows the battalion commander to position the command post in a field location and to control the simulated actions of subordinate elements in a combat scenario using organic communications equipment.

The system is a computer-driven simulator which provides real-time information about locations, activities, casualties, and capabilities of friendly and enemy units. Friendly units are maneuvered in accordance with the directions of the battalion commander and staff, while enemy units are maneuvered by a controller. The results of commander-or-controller-directed activity are simulated by the computer. Maneuvers occur over a digitized map area, allowing the computer to calculate engagement possibilities between units. Contacts are automatically determined, and casualties are assessed by computer based upon the relative dispositions and combat effectiveness of the units in contact.

ARTBASS is an improved version of the combined arms tactical training simulator, a fixed system located at the Army's Command and General Staff College in Ft. Leavenworth, Kansas. Providing more maneuver elements, a larger digitized maneuver area, and greater fidelity, the system is mounted in trailers which can be moved to the location of the unit requiring training. ARTBASS is currently entering the full-scale engineering development phase.

12.3.   TANK TRAINERS

Tank trainers typify the application of advanced technology in training devices. At the forefront of technology in visual simulation is the conduct of fire trainer (COFT) for the XM-1 and M60 tanks. These trainers apply state-of-the-art high-resolution CGI to realistically portray a combat situation. In addition, COFT represents the extension of sophisticated devices from the centralized training base to the soldier in the field.

COFT is designed to provide basic and advanced training in tank gunnery on a year-round basis at the unit level. The system consists of a gunner station, a tank commander station, and an instructor station. Modeled on the interiors of the XM-1 and M60 tanks, the gunner and commander stations provide in appearance and operation the same control mechanism and sighting equipment as are found on the tanks. COFT uses high-resolution CGI and an aural system to create the interior and exterior environment and situation with which the crew interacts (Figure 12.1).

The device permits training in operational procedures and target acquisition, identification, and engagement using either primary or secondary fire-control and sighting equipment that closely approximates the interior of a turret. This training can include conditions such as inoperable components of fire-control equipment, multiple target arrays consisting of a mix of stationary and moving targets, a variety of terrain scenes, and day, night, or reduced-visibility conditions. The instructor station provides the capability to monitor the crew's equipment, insert malfunctions, and provide feedback and scoring for performance evaluation.

The COFT trainer will be mounted in movable shelters for use at battalion level. This proximity to the unit will afford maximum opportunity for crew proficiency development and increased readiness as an important supplement to periodic live firing of the weapons.

Maintenance training, always a prime consideration for mechanized forces, is being assisted through the development and fielding of several computer-driven maintenance troubleshooting trainers. These trainers use a 2-D panel to depict one or more of the mechanical, electrical, or hydraulic systems within a vehicle. (Certain 3-D control or check points, such as switches, electrical contact points, and meters, are also on this

Figure 12.1. Scene taken from GE COFT instructor's console. The reticle and range marks are shown in the foreground as they would be seen through the trainee's viewing scope. (This photograph appears in color in the color section.)

panel.) The panel is activated by computer to provide the student the visual, mechanical, or aural feedback associated with the depicted system when it is in operation.

12.4. FLIGHT SIMULATORS

Early flight simulators were primarily instrument trainers with no visual system and a minimal motion system. But the requirement for the development of additional pilot skills, especially nap-of-the-earth flying, generated demand for a high-fidelity visual system in flight trainers.

The AH-1 flight and weapons simulator is the most recent Army helicopter trainer to complete development. This trainer consists of two cockpits, which simulate the pilot and gunner positions in the aircraft. A motion system provides roll, pitch, yaw, lateral displacement, vertical displacement, and longitudinal displacement cues. The two training stations can be used independently for individual training, or they can be electronically coupled to provide crew training. A remote instructor station containing monitoring, recording, and control equipment manages the training scenario. A computer directs the appropriate visual and motion responses and scores how well the pilot and gunner manipulate the aircraft and the armament control systems. A rudimentary CGI system has been superimposed on the modelboard presentation and provides visual cues for weapon-firing simulation.

12.5.   THE ARMY COMMITMENT

The Army is heavily committed to the use of training devices as an alternative to more traditional training on tactical equipment. The systems described here represent only a small portion of the total program for the acquisition of training devices and other aids. Since there appears to be little possibility for relief from the conditions which necessitated the commitment to this alternative training method, continued and increasing emphasis is expected for the future. As technology advances and the understanding of the factors determining training effectiveness increases, training devices should gain in acceptance not just as a substitute for operational equipment, but as the preferred means of training.

13 FLIGHT SIMULATION IN AIR-COMBAT TRAINING

RICHARD C. NEEDHAM, BERNELL J. EDWARDS, JR., AND DIRK C. PRATHER

The mission of the Air Force is to fly and fight. Providing essential support to the accomplishment of this mission is the Operations Training Division of the Air Force Human Resources Laboratory. Established in 1969, the division applies the best available scientific knowledge and technology to make Air Force operations training as effective as possible.

Within the Operations Training Division are two units that develop and test technology applicable to operational training. The engineering research and development unit provides the hardware systems for training; the behavioral-science research and development unit develops methods for making hardware better fit the user's needs.

During the early and middle 1970s, operations training research focused on part-task trainers that demonstrated the potential for using simulators for undergraduate pilot training. A series of laboratory studies revealed that a great deal of time could be saved in both the instrument and the contact phases of training without adversely affecting the pilot's performance.

The instrument flight simulator now used for undergraduate pilot training is an outgrowth of these studies. Affirming the instrument flight simulator's value in reducing training time, a study involving 1750 undergraduate pilots revealed an annual savings of no less than 90,000 flying hours and 25 million gallons of fuel.

In 1975 a more sophisticated simulator, the advanced simulator for pilot training (ASPT), was produced. It was originally designed to be a state-of-the-art simulator that could be used to develop and test technology as a procurement guide. To date, however, it has been used as a test bed for identifying the specific capabilities a training device must have if it is to offer effective training in particular tasks.

The ASPT has two 6-degree-of-freedom motion platforms. Aircraft flight dynamics and control loading characteristics are computer-programmable for both the motion and the visual systems. The visual display is computer generated through a 7-channel CRT system, which provides a 300° horizontal by 140° vertical field of view. The instructor interacts with the student pilot via an operator console that allows the instructor to manipulate a variety of training conditions and task elements.

An early concern in testing ASPT involved the relative contribution of platform motion to training effectiveness. Simulator platform motion is an expensive item, and its costs must be justified in terms of benefits gained. Over the past several years a number of studies of platform motion have indicated that platform motion does not improve training, suggesting that simulation dollars are perhaps better spent on visual systems and on research in other areas. Evaluations of ASPT have generated sufficient data to predict simulator requirements for given transfer effectiveness ratios in certain task areas. These include:

Normal procedures.
Emergency procedures.
Instrument flight.
Aerial refueling.
Takeoff.
Landing approach.
Close formation.

At present more research is needed to define simulation requirements in the areas of:

Air-to-air tasks.
Air-to-surface weapons delivery.
Low-level navigation and advanced weapons delivery.
Tactical formation.
Force cue requirements for pilot-induced gravity-force cuing and externally induced disturbance.

Thus far the ASPT has demonstrated that relatively low-fidelity simulation training can transfer effectively to air-to-ground weapons delivery skills.

A study of F-5B pilot training was the first effort directly supporting tactical pilot training and marked the beginning of a trend toward collaboration with the Tactical Air Command in training and research efforts.

In the F-5B study, recent pilot training graduates were the subjects. Half of the subjects, the experimental group, received air-to-ground mission training in the ASPT; the other half, the control group, did not receive simulator training. Both groups flew an actual air-to-ground mission in the F-5B with an instructor pilot in the back seat for safety purposes. The simulator-trained experimental group performed better than their counterparts in the control group in all tasks (Figure 13.1).

The ongoing effort in A-10 simulation development is really an extension of the earlier F-5B study. In the A-10 training, several experiments in initial air-to-ground training produced some interesting results. Again, a transfer-of-training paradigm was used. An experimental group received three air-to-ground training missions in the A-10 simulator. In the strafe

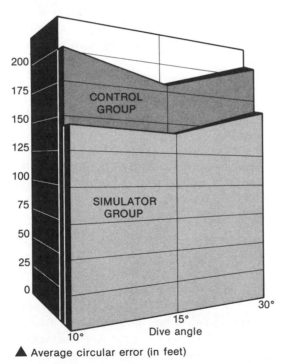

Figure 13.1. The effect of simulator training on air-to-surface delivery performance in the F-5B aircraft.

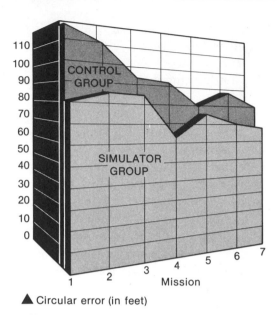

Figure 13.2. The effect of simulator training on air-to-surface performance in the A-10 aircraft.

task, the experimental group outscored the control group on all five missions (Figure 13.2).

In the dive-bomb task, the experimental group's circular error was better on all seven missions (Figure 13.3). This is the first study to demonstrate the durability of simulator training. Earlier studies suggested that the effects of simulator training disappeared after two or three missions. Here these effects were still evident after seven flights.

Results from previous A-10 research of limited air-to-ground weapon deliveries suggested the feasibility of extending weapon-delivery training to a simulated combat environment. Existing ASPT visual models were modified to depict a 10-square-mile hostile environment, with hills of various elevations and strategically placed antiaircraft and surface-to-air missiles. An air-defense system was modeled so that an A-10's penetration of a surface-to-air missile firing envelope activated the missile. Warning tones associated with missile acquisition and launch were provided to the pilot. The target was a tank that could be located at six randomly selected positions on a road. It had no offensive capability and was considered destroyed by one round from the A-10 cannon.

Combat-ready A-10 pilots participated in the evaluation.They flew a mission in which they entered the combat area, attempted to destroy the tank while evading hostile fire, and egressed the area. Pilots flew 20 runs.

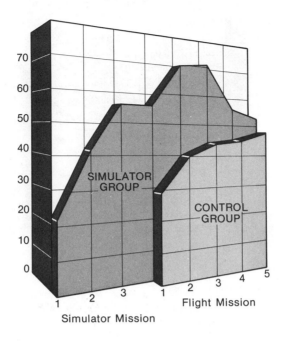

▲ Percent of rounds through target

Figure 13.3. The effect of simulator training on low-angle strafe performance in the A-10 aircraft.

Each run was terminated as a result of one of the following:

Surface-to-air mission kill.

Antiaircraft artillery kill.

Terrain crash.

Overstress.

Safe egress across the forward edge of the battle area.

The pilots were briefed on the capability of the air-defense threat and were given a map of the threat location. The antiaircraft guns had a kill probability of 100 percent if the pilot allowed the gun to achieve a tracking solution for 6 seconds. Activated surface-to-air missiles could be evaded with proper maneuvering.

Performance results were analyzed on the basis of whether the pilot hit or missed the target, survived, or was destroyed. All participants showed progressively improved performance in offensive and defensive skills (Figure 13.4). After terrain crash and overstress losses were removed from

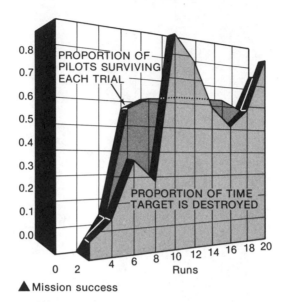

Figure 13.4.   Survivability and attack learning curves of A-10 pilots operating in a simulated combat environment.

the results of the first two runs, the learning curves were similar to those of actual combat, indicating that this kind of training should improve pilots' survivability, particularly during their first few combat missions.

Judging from these results, there seems to be no apparent reason why combat scenarios cannot be modeled for simulation training. If losses in the first few missions of a war can be decreased through the expanded use of simulation, then this type of training is, in effect, a force multiplier.

Another part of A-10-related research and development addresses the use of the ASPT for the A-10 manual reversion flight control system (MRFCS) and a degraded flight control mode. At present this training is not done in the actual aircraft because of the safety risk.

The results are clear-cut. The manual reversion mode is trainable through simulation, and it appears likely that a simulator-trained pilot can fly a battle-damaged aircraft deftly enough to safely land or eject. Some specifics in the data show that a wide field of view in the simulator results in better pilot performance for this task, and that the more complex the failure mode, the poorer the pilot performance. Moreover, the presence or absence of platform motion does not appear to affect performance in any failure condition. Indeed, there can be little doubt that this manual-reversion example reflects the value of simulators in teaching those maneuvers that cannot be taught safely in the aircraft.

The F-16 simulator development program is another major project being undertaken for the Tactical Air Command. A basic F-16 simulation has been built into ASPT so that the Tactical Air Command can have simulator training for F-16 pilots before the operational F-16 simulator is delivered. There are several high-priority research-and-development issues being addressed in this program. These include the impact on training of simulated turbulence and the effectiveness of wide-field-of-view simulation for F-16 initial transition and air-to-ground weapons tasks.

Another important ongoing effort is Project SMART (skills maintenance and reacquisition training). This effort is central to the Air Force's commitment to maintaining adequate aircrew readiness with minimal use of energy resources. The thrust of SMART is the objective measurement of flying skills. To date, development of skill measures has been directed toward B-52 aircrew proficiencies, primarily crew coordination, task analysis, and radar bombing skills.

Simulators have been used mainly for transition and instrument training. Air Force units with simulators have used them as substitute aircraft for a portion of their training programs. With the advent of sophisticated full-field-of-view simulators, interactive training scenarios between geographically separated units can be composed.

The Air Force's long-range goal is the development of a high-technology base for air-combat training through simulated combat environments. The target date is fiscal year 1987. As this technology evolves, it is expected that the products—hardware and methodology—will transfer to user commands.

Of course, the final test of training effectiveness is crew performance in combat: the better the training, the better the aircrew performance and survivability. The high cost of the first 10 days of war is well reflected in projected aircrew and aircraft attrition figures. Three shortcomings in training opportunities are generally cited as contributors to this early attrition. These are:

1. Inability of aircrews to practice maneuvers for evading surface-to-air missiles.

2. Omission of actual antiaircraft artillery fire or field-launched heat-seeking missiles from bombing and strafing practice.

3. Lack of threat-aircraft replication in the aircrew training environment.

Certainly, in light of the expectation of high attrition in the first week of combat, a training device that introduced aircrews to the combat situation and that permitted them to practice critical skills under the stress of engagement would be tremendously valuable. It appears to be a matter of only several years before such a training simulator can be developed. In the 1980s, air-combat training technology will focus on the reduction of first-mission attrition. It is hoped that this technology will also permit units to predict levels of combat readiness using empirical data.

Most flying tasks are composed of various visual-skill components. Consequently it is very important to identify and define visual cue requirements for air-combat training. In fact, because of its great impact on training cost and effectiveness, it may well be the single most important research area. Although the low-altitude flight task has been identified as the most demanding combat training problem, visual simulation in this area is quite limited because of the high level of visual detail required. The training requirements for the visual tasks associated with the low-altitude environment must be identified and developed before full-mission simulation can be achieved.

As work in CIG proceeds, behavioral researchers and engineers will be testing the training value of various visual-system improvements, such as increased scene detail, dynamic modeling of the environment, texture, and color. This technology development and testing will be pursued in a number of areas as hardware state-of-the-art progresses.

The full development of a simulated hostile environment is the goal. It will help the Air Force groom better combat-ready pilots. It will spur development of low-altitude flight skills through visual nap-of-the-earth simulation. Moreover, it will provide a test bed for measuring combat performance, and it may even lead to the merging of simulated air and ground operations.

As CIG advances, a new nontraditional concept of fidelity seems to be emerging. In combat simulation those quantifiable variables known to affect the outcome of engagements are of the greatest importance. Several areas of development are now being considered for the expanded-combat simulation model.

Of high priority is visual-terrain simulation. A-10 close-air-support training will require the best representation available. The data base should offer a suitable likeness of European and Mideastern terrain. The Defense Mapping Agency has digitized data bases for these areas, and the Army is considering using them for its armor full-crew research simulator.

The visual simulation of maneuver elements on the ground is also very important. It should depict both friendly and hostile forces in the forward edge of the battle area and should impose the A-10 close-air-support scenario over a preprogrammed ground battle. The battle scale should be on the order of two enemy tank regiments against one reinforced friendly tank battalion. This scale corresponds to a reasonable level of simulation for close-air-support engagements.

Moving models should be included in a pilot's visual scene. A single moving model could represent unit movement as the aircraft was in the distance. As it got closer to the battle, movement of individual companies could be visually represented with several models. Then, when the A-10 was within attack range, moving models would represent individual vehicles.

Experimentation is needed to define precise limits for this order of simulation. Visual feedback for training will be important. The system should have a lookback or reverse display so that the pilots can see how their aircraft appear from ground positions.

For battle scenarios it is foreseen that the instructor will be able to select the presence of specific weapons, their position and firing characteristics, engagement strategies, the effect of smoke, and other elements affecting battle interaction programmed as hit probabilities. For instance, the A-10, when hit by antiaircraft artillery fire, might go into a manual-reversion mode. The suppressive effects of air-to-ground fire would also be provided, altering the firing probabilities of ground units.

Active and preprogrammed control of tactical aircraft other than those piloted would be available, as would all communication modes between them. An instructor or operator would be able to position weapons on the ground using a light pen and CRT display. This will yield the feedback the operator needs to set up a fire plan and position weapons for a combat scenario. The graphics system will permit the operator to zoom in on specific areas. In addition the system will have on-line 3-D playback that will provide a visual trace of the flight path, aircraft-state parameters, and threat envelopes. Graphics playback would feature slow-motion and freeze modes.

Future engineering efforts in the training equipment area will focus on immediate and long-range improvements to the ASPT and on the advancement of visual-simulation technology. Projected improvements to the ASPT will include modularization of aircraft types for rapid cockpit changeovers, including programmable control loading and flight dynamics and provisions for manual-reversion simulation. The visual data base for the ASPT will be modernized to include moving ground models, increased edge capacity, and quadric solid generation. In addition, helmet mounted sensors and displays will be used to better convey the imagery to the pilot.

These improvements are interim steps toward a comprehensive engagement-simulation technology that will support full-mission combat training. Indeed, forthcoming engineering and behavioral research and development will make it possible for aircrews to train under conditions that truly approach actual combat conditions.

14 TRAINING CENTERS FOR BUSINESS AIRCRAFT

BRUCE J. SCHACHTER

FlightSafety International operates 23 learning centers for pilots, including one in Canada and two in Europe. Its fleet of simulators covers aircraft manufactured by 15 different companies, and includes over 50 visual systems (Figure 14.1). The major source of company revenue is from the

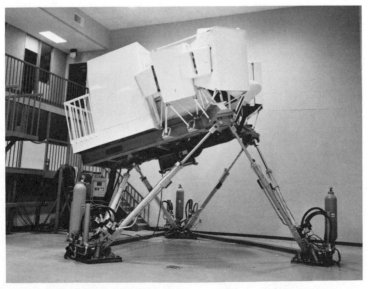

Figure 14.1. FlightSafety's Bell helicopter flight simulator with 6-degree-of-freedom motion platform and color visual system.

training of crews for high-performance turboprop and turbojet business aircraft. Since sale of these aircraft types is increasing at a steady rate, FlightSafety expects its operation to grow. FlightSafety also operates an academy in Vero Beach, Florida, which trains 500 students annually. Its courses take students from primary training in single-engine aircraft, through commercial multiengine, instrument, and air-transport ratings.

Until recently there was no real competition to FlightSafety International for training pilots for business aircraft, since no one but the airlines and the military was prepared to spend the millions required to set up a fleet of simulators. But recently a company called SimuFlite was formed. It is receiving $35 million in startup funds from Singer Company. Its operations in Dallas will begin with 12 Singer/Miles Image-II dusk/night visual systems. SimuFlite's training program will emphasize semiannual review and refresher courses.

Embry-Riddle Aeronautical University of Daytona Beach, Florida, offers an academic curriculum directed toward aviation careers. It has recently purchased visual simulators manufactured by Aviation Simulation Technology for training students for multiengine aircraft.

BIBLIOGRAPHY

AIRM79   *Airman's Information Manual*, Aero Publ. Co., Fallbrook, CA, 1979. (Covers navigation lighting and marking aids.)

AKIN77   A. D. Akinde, R. L. Grimsdale, A. A. Hadjislanis, P. J. Willis, and D. J. Woollons, "The Use of a Surface Oriented Color Raster Display in Computer Image Generation of Images for Flight Simulation," in *Proc. IEE Conf. on Displays for Man-Machine Systems* (Lancaster, England, April 4–7, 1977), M. W. Bailey, 1977, pp. 1–5.

ANDE77   P. R. Anderson, "An Analysis of a Hidden Line and Surface Algorithm in Terms of Hardware," M.S. Thesis, University of Illinois, Computer Science Dept., Urbana, 1977.

AVIA70   "Radar Cockpit Views Simulated," *Aviat. Week and Space Technol.*, pp. 46–50 (June 8, 1970).

BADL79   N. I. Badler and S. W. Smoliar, "Digital Representations of Human Movement," *ACM Comput. Surv.*, **11**(1), pp. 19–38 (March 1979).

BARO78   E. C. Baron and P. E. Sprotbery, "Liquid Crystal Light Valve Projectors for Simulation Applications," in SPIE, vol. 162: *Visual Simulation and Image Realism*, 1978, pp. 138–143.

BEAR77   H. Beardsley, W. M. Bunker, A. Eibeck, J. Juhlin, W. Kelly, J. Page, and L. Shaffer, "Advanced Simulation in Undergraduate Pilot Training (ASUPT): Computer Image Generation," AFHRL-TR-75-59(V), for Air Force Human Resource Lab., Wright Patterson AFB, OH, by General Electric Co., Daytona Beach, FL, November 1977. (Describes GE ASUPT system in great depth.)

BENN75   W. S. Bennett, "Computer Generated Graphics: A Review of Some of the More Well Known Methods Applicable to Simulation," in SPIE, vol. 59: *Simulators and Simulation*, 1975, pp. 3–11.

BLAC77   S. R. Black, "Digital Processing of 3-D Data to Generate Interactive Real-Time Dynamic Pictures," in SPIE, vol. 120: *Three-Dimensional Imaging*, 1977, pp. 52–61.

221

BLEH78   W. P. Bleha, L. T. Lipton, E. Wiener-Avnear, J. Grinberg, P. G. Reif, D. Casasent, H. B. Brown, and B. V. Markevitch, "Application of the Liquid Crystal Light Valve to Real-Time Optical Data Processing," *Opt. Eng.*, **17**(4), 371–384 (July–August 1978).

BROW73   J. L. Brown, "Visual Elements in Flight Simulation," TR 73-2, University of Rochester Center for Visual Sciences, Rochester, NY, December 1973.

BROW77   R. F. Browning, L. E. Ryan, P. G. Scott, and A. F. Smode, "Training Effectiveness Evaluation of Device 2F87F, P-3C Operational Flight Trainer," Rep. 42, Training and Evaluation Group, Naval Training Equipment Center, Orlando, FL, January 1977.

BROW78   R. F. Browning, L. E. Ryan, and P. G. Scott, "Utilization of Device 2F87F OFT to Achieve Flight Hour Reduction in P-3 Fleet Replacement Training," Rep. 54, Training and Evaluation Group, Naval Training Equipment Center, Orlando, FL, April 1978.

BUNK72   W. M. Bunker, "Visual Scene Simulation with Computer Generated Images," in *Proc. 5th Annual Simulation Symp.: Progress in Simulation*, Gordon and Breach, New York, 1972, pp. 91–114.

BUNK73a   W. M. Bunker, "Techniques for Simulation of Radar Displays," in *Proc. 6th Annual Simulation Symp.* (Tampa, FL, March 7–9, 1973), pp. 1–25.

BUNK73b   W. M. Bunker, "Real Time, Three-Dimensional Visual Scene Generation with Computer Generated Imagery," in *Proc. Summer Computer Simulation Conf.* (Montreal, July 13–15, 1973), pp. 205–212.

BUNK73c   W. M. Bunker, "Image Quality Improvement in Computed Visual Scene Simulation," in *Proc. 6th Naval Training Equip. Center/ Industry Conf.* (Orlando, FL, November 13–15, 1973), pp. 96–124.

BUNK74   W. M. Bunker, "The Simulation Data Base—Describing the World to the Computer," in *Proc. Summer Computer Simulation Conf.* (Houston, TX, July 8–11, 1974), pp. 55–84.

BUNK75   W. M. Bunker and R. Heartz, "Perspective Display Simulation of Terrain," AFHRL F33615-75-C-5243, Air Force Human Resource Lab., Wright Patterson AFB, OH, 1975. (Original derivation of algorithm for displaying grid data bases in perspective.)

BUNK76   W. M. Bunker, "Computer Generated Images Simulate Infrared and Low Light Level Television Displays," in *Proc. AIAA Visual and Motion Simulation Conf.* (Dayton, OH, April 1976), pp. 120–132.

BUNK77a   W. M. Bunker, "Computer Generation of Images—The Multi-Purpose Tool," in SPIE, vol. 59: *Simulators and Simulation*, March 1977, pp. 25–39.

BUNK77b   W. M. Bunker, "Computer Simulation of Electro-Optical Viewing Systems," *J. Aircraft*, **14**(4), pp. 394–440 (April 1977).

BUNK77c   W. M. Bunker and N. E. Ferris, "Computer Image Generation— Imagery Improvement: Circles, Contours, and Texture," TR-77-66, Air Force Human Resource Lab., Air Force Systems Command,

Brooks AFB, TX, September 1977. (Original report on feasibility of real-time texture generation and real-time display of objects with curved surfaces.)

BUNK78   W. M. Bunker, "Training Effectiveness vs. Simulation Realism," in *Proc. 11th Industry Conf.* (Orlando, FL, November 1978).

BUNK79a   W. M. Bunker and R. F. Pester, "Computer Image Generation: Improved Edge Utilization Study," AFHRL-TR-78-81, Air Force Human Resource Lab., Wright Patterson AFB, OH, February 1979. (Discusses level of detail concept for data bases.)

BUNK79b   W. M. Bunker, "CIG Translucent Face Simulation Provides Multiple Benefits," in *Proc. 1st Interservice/Industry Training Equipment Conf.* (Orlando, FL, November 27–29, 1979), pp. 229–237.

CATM74   E. Catmull, "A Subdivision Algorithm for Computer Display of Curved Surfaces, University of Utah Computer Science Dept., TR 74-133, December 1974.

CATM79   E. Catmull, "A Hidden-Surface Algorithm with Anti-Aliasing," *Comput. Graphics*, pp. 6–10 (1979).

CHEN75   W. L. Chen, "Night Calligraphic Digital Visual System," in SPIE, vol. 59: *Simulators and Simulation*, 1975, pp. 40–47.

CLAR80   J. Clark, "A VLSI Geometry Processor for Graphics," *Computer*, pp. 59–69 (July 1980).

CLAR82   J. Clark, "The Geometry Engine: A VLSI Geometry System for Graphics," *Comput. Graphics*, **16**(3), pp. 127–133 (July 1982).

COHE80   D. Cohen and S. Demetrescu, "A VLSI Approach to Computer Image Generation," Tech. Rep., University of Southern California, Information Sciences Inst., Los Angeles, 1980.

COLL78   S. C. Collyer and W. S. Chambers, "AWAVS: A Research Facility for Defining Flight Training Visual System Requirements," in *Proc. 1978 Human Factors Society 22nd Annual Meeting*, pp. 99–107.

CONR80   Conrac Corporation, *Raster Graphics Handbook*, 1980.

CORO80   J. T. Corollo and N. D. Reynolds, "Distortion Correction in Computer Image Generation Based Wide Angle Visual Display System," in *Proc. 2nd Interservice/Industry Training Equipment Conf.* (Salt Lake City, UT, November 18–20, 1980), pp. 29–36. (Discusses distortion correction for a dome display system.)

CROC68   C. P. Crocetti, E. J. Calucci, A. D. Rugari, and C. M. Blank, "Light Valves, Lasers, and Electroluminescent Devices," in *Display Systems Engineering*, H. R. Luxenberg and R. L. Kueh, Eds., McGraw-Hill, New York, 1968, pp. 319–391.

CROW77   F. Crow, "The Aliasing Problem in Computer-Generated Shaded Images," *Commun. ACM*, **20**(11), pp. 799–805 (November 1977).

CUNN80   T. B. Cunningham and G. O. Picasso, "Automation of Data Base Development in Computer Image Generators," in *Proc. 2nd Interservice/Industry Training Equipment Conf.* (Salt Lake City, UT, November 18–20, 1980), pp. 17–21.

DEFE80   Special issue on "Simulation Research and Applications," *Defense Manage. J.* **16**(4), Fourth Quarter 1980, publ. by the Office of the Assistant Secretary of Defense (Manpower Reserve Affairs and Logistics), Journal Office: OASD (MRA&L), Cameron Station, Alexandria, VA.

DICH80   W. Dichter, K. Doris, and C. Conkling, "A New Approach to CGI Systems," in *Proc. 2nd Interservice/Industry Training Equipment Conf.* (Salt Lake City, UT, November 18–20, 1980), pp. 102–109.

DICH81   W. Dichter, K. Doris, and C. Conklin, "A Raster Scan CIG System Based on Refresh Memory," presented at 25th SPIE Conference (San Diego, CA, August 1981).

DOCT81   L. J. Doctor and J. G. Torborg, "Display Techniques for Octree-Encoded Objects," *IEEE Comput. Graphics*, **1**(3), pp. 20–40 (1981).

EDDO80   E. E. Eddowes and W. L. Waag, "The Use of Simulators for Training for In-Flight and Emergency Procedures," Rep. 248, NATO Advisory Group for Research and Development, Neuilly-sur-Seine, France, June 1980. (Also U.S. Air Force Human Resource Lab., Williams AFB, AZ.)

ELEC67   "Right Perspective," *Electron. Rev.*, pp. 43–44 (October 16, 1967). (Briefly covers GE NASA 240 edge system.)

ELSO76   B. M. Elson, "Simulators Slash Pilot Training Time," *Aviat. Week and Space Technol.*, pp. 59–61 (October 4, 1976).

ELSO81   B. M. Elson, "Boeing Studies New Imagery Technique," *Aviat. Week and Space Technol.*, pp. 78–85 (December 14, 1981).

ERDA72   A. C. Erdahl, "Displaying Computer Generated Half-Tone Pictures in Real Time," RADC-TR-250, University of Utah, Computer Science Dept., 1972, for Rome Air Development Center, Rome, NY.

ERDA78   A. C. Erdahl, "Improved Scene Generator Capability," NASA NAS-9-14010, Evans and Sutherland Computer Co., October 1978.

EVAN   Evans and Sutherland Computer Company's annual reports and calendars.

FEIB80   E. Feibush, M. Levoy, and R. Cook, "Synthetic Texturing Using Digital Filters," *Comput. Graphics*, **14**(3), pp. 294–301 (July 1980).

FLIG78   "Airliner Simulation Census," *Flight Int.*, pp. 438–439 (February 18, 1978).

FOLE79   W. L. Foley, "Real-Time Simulation of FLIR and LLLTV Systems for Aircrew Training," in *Proc. 10th Annual Pittsburgh Conf. on Modeling and Simulation* (Pittsburgh, PA, 1979), pp. 1737–1746.

FOLE82   J. D. Foley and A. Van Dam, *Fundamentals of Interactive Computer Graphics*, Addison-Wesley, Reading, MA, 1982.

FORB78   J. E. Forbes, "The Stress Is Now Toward Better Training in Less Space at Lower Cost," *ICAO Bull.*, pp. 22–25 (April 1978).

FUCH79a   H. Fuchs, "An Expandable Multiprocessor Architecture for Video Graphics," Tech. Rep. 79-002, University of North Carolina, Chapel Hill, 1979.

FUCH79b   H. Fuchs and Z. M. Kedem, "Predetermining Visibility Priority in 3-D Scenes," *Proc. SIGGRAPH,* **13**(2), pp. 175–181 (August 1979).

FUCH81   H. Fuchs and B. W. Johnson, "An Expandable Multiprocessor Architecture for Video Graphics," in *Proc. 6th Annual ACM IEEE Symp. on Computer Architecture,* 1981, pp. 20–28.

GARD78   G. Y. Gardner, "Computer Image Generation of Curved Objects for Simulator Displays," in *Proc. 11th Naval Training Equipment Center/Industry Conf.* (Orlando, FL, November 1978), pp. 7-9 to 7-14.

GARD79a   G. Y. Gardner and E. P. Berlin, "Effective Antialiasing of Computer Generated Images," in *Proc. 2nd Interservice/Industry Training Equipment Conf.* (Salt Lake City, UT, November 18–20, 1980), pp. 22–25.

GARD79b   G. Y. Gardner, "Computer Generated Texturing to Model Real World Features," in *Proc. 1st Interservice/Industry Training Equipment Conf.* (Orlando, FL, November 27–29, 1979), pp. 239–245.

GE66   *Instruction Manual for Digital Contact Analog, vol. A: Theory, Operation, and Maintenance,* for Joint Army/Navy Instrumentation Research Program by General Electric Co., Electronics Lab., Contract NR 4057[00], Syracuse, NY, May 1966.

GE   *Instruction Manual for Visual Three-View Space-Flight Simulator,* part 1, vol. A, for NASA Manned Spacecraft Center, Houston, TX, by General Electric Co., Advanced Electronics Center, Contract NAS 9-1375, Ithaca, NY, undated.

GIBS55   J. J. Gibson, P. Olum, and F. Rosenblatt, "Parallax and Perspective During Aircraft Landings," *Am. J. Psychol.,* **68**, pp. 372–385 (1955).

GILL80   F. Gillard, "A Realistic Aim or an Expensive Luxury?" *ICAO Bull.,* pp. 35–37 (April 1980).

GILL72   M. G. Gilliland, "Status of Computer Generated Imagery for Visual Simulation," in *Proc. 5th Naval Training Equipment Conf.* (Orlando, FL, February 1972), pp. 175–180.

GOOD75   W. E. Good, "Recent Advances in Single-Gun Television Light Valve Projectors," in SPIE, vol. 59: *Simulators and Simulation,* 1975, pp. 96–99.

GOUR71   H. Gouraud, "Computer Display of Curved Surfaces," TR 113, University of Utah, Computer Science Dept., June 1971.

GRAN78   M. S. K. Grant, "Day, Dusk, and Night Visuals Are Here, But Cost and Image Quality Are Trade-off Considerations," *ICAO Bull.,* pp. 12–16 (April 1978).

GUM79   D. R. Gum and A. T. Gill, "Visual Simulation Image Input Devices," sec. 9.4 of notes for *Flight Simulator Short Course* (Dayton, OH, 1979). (An excellent review.)

GUND77   A. J. Gundry and J. M. Rolfe, "Human Factors Topics in Flight Simulation: An Annotated Bibliography," Rep. 656, NATO Advisory Group for Research and Development, Neuilly-sur-Seine, France, June 1977.

GUNW75   R. L. Gunwaldsen, "CHARGE Image Generator: Theory of Operation and Author Language Support," TR 75-3, Human Resources Research Org., Alexandria, VA, May 1975.

GUPT81   S. Gupta, R. F. Sproull, and I. E. Sutherland, "A VLSI Architecture for Updating Raster Scan Displays," *Proc. SIGGRAPH*, **15**(3), pp. 71–78 (August 1981).

HAND75   G. O. Handberg, "Computer Generated Imagery Has Sparked a Revolution in Visual Simulation," *ICAO Bull.*, pp. 29–32 (October 1975).

HAND77   G. O. Handberg, "Advanced CGI Visual Technology Reshapes Pilot Training Possibilities," *ICAO Bull.*, pp. 27–32 (April 1977).

HART80   N. R. Hartley, "A New Challenge: Flight Training in the 1980s," *ICAO Bull.*, pp. 30–37 (1980).

HAYW78   D. Hayworth, "Airborne Electro-Optical Sensor Simulation System," AFHRL-TR-78-41, Air Force Human Resource Lab., Wright Patterson AFB, OH, August 1978.

HEAR71   R. A. Heartz and W. M. Bunker, "Radar Display Simulation for Training," *Analog/Hybrid Comput. Educ. Soc. Trans.*, **3**(6), pp. 109–120, June 1971.

HEAR72   R. A. Heartz, "Digital Radar Landmass Simulation," in *Proc. 5th Naval Center and Industry Conf.* (Orlando, FL, February 15–17, 1972), pp. 50–57.

HEND49   C. D. Hendley and S. Hect, "The Colors of Natural Terrain and Their Relation to Visual Color Deficiencies," *J. Opt. Soc. Am.*, **39**(10), pp. 870–873 (1949).

HEND75   H. C. Hendrickson and J. D. Stafford, "Television Projectors," in *SPIE*, vol. 59: *Simulators and Simulation*, 1975, pp. 88–95.

HIRS78   M. Hirst, "The Big New World of Military Simulators," *Flight Int.*, pp. 1951–1957 (November 25, 1978).

HOLM79   G. L. Holman, "Training Effectiveness of the CH-47 Flight Simulator," Res. Rep. 1209, U.S. Army Research Institute, May 1979.

ISLE74   R. N. Isley, W. E. Corley, and P. W. Caro, "The Development of U.S. Coast Guard Aviation Synthetic Equipment and Training Programs," Air Force Human Resources Research Org., Wright Patterson AFB, OH, October 1974.

JACK80   J. H. Jackson, "Dynamic Scan-Converted Images with a Frame Buffer Display Device," *Comput. Graphics*, **14**(3), pp. 163–169 (July 1980).

KAPL79   M. Kaplan and D. Greenberg, "Parallel Processing Techniques for Hidden Surface Removal," *Comput. Graphics*, **13**, pp. 300–307 (1979).

KART80   S. P. Kartashev and S. I. Kartashev, Ed., special issue on "Supersystems for the '80s," *IEEE Computer*, **13**(11) (November 1980).

KASH78   E. F. Kashork and J. A. Turner, "Aviation Wide Angle Visual System (AWAVS): Visual Performance," in *Proc. SPIE Conf.* (San Diego, CA, August 30, 1978), pp. 36–39.

KOGG81   P. M. Kogg, *Architecture of Pipelined Computers*, McGraw-Hill, New York, 1981.

KOON79   J. M. Koonce, "Predictive Validity of Flight Simulators as a Function of Simulator Motion," *Human Factors*, **21**, pp. 215–223 (1979).

KOTA78   J. Kotas and J. L. Booker, "The AWAVS Data Facility—A Comprehensive Preparation Package," in *Proc. 11th Naval Training Equipment Center/Industry Conf.* (Orlando, FL, November 1978), pp. 49–62.

KRAF80   C. L. Kraft, C. D. Anderson, and C. E. Elevorti, "Pilot Performance as a Function of Peripheral Cues and Color in Computer Generated Imagery," in *Proc. 1980 Summer Computer Simulation Conf.* (Seattle, WA, August 25–27), pp. 383–385.

LARU78   J. A. LaRussa and A. T. Gill, "The Holographic Pancake Window™," in SPIE, vol. 162: *Visual Simulation and Image Realism*, 1978, pp. 120–129.

LARU79   J. A. LaRussa, "Visual Display Systems," sec. 9.3 of notes for *Flight Simulation Short Course* (Dayton, OH, 1979). (An excellent review.)

LEE80   D. T. Lee and B. J. Schachter, "Two Algorithms for Constructing a Delaunay Triangulation," *Int. J. Comput. and Inf. Sci.*, **9**(3), pp. 219–242 (June 1980).

LEMA78   W. D. LeMaster and T. M. Longridge, "Area of Interest Field-of-View Research Using ASPT," AFHRL-TR-78-11, Air Force Human Resource Lab., Williams AFB, AZ, May 1978.

LEWA80   F. P. Lewandowski, D. Hinkle, and W. Tucker, "Digital Visual Special Effects," in *Proc. 2nd Interservice/Industry Training Equipment Conf.* (Salt Lake City, UT, November 18–20, 1980), pp. 84–91.

LUCE73   L. Luce, "VITAL II," *Shell Aviat. News*, pp. 26–29 (1973).

LUDV81   E. C. Ludvigsen, "Combat in a Box," *Army*, **31**(8), pp. 14–21 (August 1981).

MAGA78   J. R. Magarinos, "Holographic Volume Phase, 17 Inch Aperture, Off-Axis, Spherical Beam Splitter Mirror," AFHRL-TR-78-29, for Air Force Human Resource Lab., Wright-Patterson AFB, OH, by Ferrand Optical Co., August 1978.

MARK75   D. M. Mark, "Computer Analysis of Topography: A Comparison of Terrain Storage Methods," *Geografiska Annaler*, **3**(4), ser. A, pp. 179–188 (1975).

MARK79   D. M. Mark, "Phenomenon-Based Data-Structuring and Digital Terrain Modeling," *Geo-Processing*, **1**, pp. 27–36 (1979).

MARR77   P. Marr and L. Shaffer, "Multichannel Wide-Angle Computer Generated Visual System," in *Proc. 10th NTEC/Industry Conf.* (Orlando, FL, November 1977), pp. 135–146. (Describes GE AWAVS system.)

MCCA70   S. McCallister and I. E. Sutherland, "Final Report on the Warnock Hidden-Line Algorithm," Evans & Sutherland Co., Salt Lake City, UT, February 1970.

MEAD79   C. Mead and L. Conway, *Introduction to VLSI Systems*, Addison-Wesley, Reading, MA, 1979.

MILI80   "F-18 Tactics Trainer," *Mil. Electron./Countermeasures*, pp. 55–56 (November 1980).

MONR78   E. G. Monroe, K. L. Mehrer, R. L. Engel, S. Hannan, J. McHugh, G. Turnage, and D. R. Lee, "Advanced Simulator for Pilot Training: Aerial Refueling Visual Simulation Engineering Development," AFHRL-78-51, Air Force Human Resource Lab., Williams AFB, AZ, September 1978.

NATO78   *Proc. Specialists Meeting of the Flight Mechanics Panel on Piloted Aircraft Environment Simulation Techniques* (Brussels, Belgium, October 24–27, 1978), AGARD CP-249 (also NTIS HC A14/MFA01), NATO Advisory Group for Aerospace Research and Development, Neuilly-sur-Seine, France.

NEWM79   W. M. Newman and R. F. Sproull, *Principles of Interactive Computer Graphics*, McGraw-Hill, New York, 1979.

OCON73   F. E. O'Conner, B. J. Shinn, and W. M. Bunker, "Prospects, Problems, and Performance: A Case Study of the First Pilot Training Device Using CGI Visuals," TIS Class 1 - 73ASD005, General Electric Co., Daytona Beach, FL, 1973.

PAPA77   R. Papapetros, "The Design of a Color Display System for Real Time Animation Using Microprocessors," M. Eng. Thesis, McGill University, Montreal, Canada, 1977.

PARK78   F. I. Parke, "The Case Shaded Graphics System," Rep. CES 79-12, Case Institute of Technology, Computer and Engineering Science Dept., Case Western Reserve University, Cleveland, OH, May 1978. (Describes E&S CT-1.)

PARK80   F. I. Parke, "Simulation and Expected Performance Analysis of Multiple Processor Z-Buffer Systems," *Comput. Graphics*, **14**(3), pp. 48–56 (July 1980).

PAVL77   T. Pavlidis, *Structural Pattern Recognition*, Springer-Verlag, New York, 1977.

PEAR75   D. E. Pearson, *Transmission and Display of Pictorial Information*, Wiley, New York, 1975.

POVE73   H. K. Povenmire and S. N. Roscoe, "Incremental Transfer Effectiveness of a Ground-Based Aviation Trainer," *Human Factors*, **15**, pp. 534–542 (1973).

PRIT80   A. G. M. Pritchett, "Animation by Computer in the Film and Television Industries," *Computer Graphics '80*, On line Pub., Middlesex, England, pp. 549–563.

RAIK76   R. R. Raike, "COMPUSCENE Modular Approach to Day-Night Simulation," in *Proc. AIAA Visual Motion and Simulation Conf.* (Dayton, OH, April 1976), pp. 101–120. (Describes approach taken in GE third-generation systems.)

RAMJ79   A. S. Ramji, "A Color Graphics Display System for Real-Time Animation Using Microprocessors," M. Eng. Thesis, McGill University, Montreal, Canada, 1979.

RANJ80a   S. E. Ranjbaran and R. J. Swallow, "COMPUTROL in Flight Simulation," in *Proc. Eurographics '80 Conf.* (Geneva, Switzerland, September 5, 1980), North-Holland, New York, 1980, pp. 321–329.

RANJ80b   S. E. Ranjbaran, "A Mathematical Model for the Visual World," in *Proc. 11th Annual Conf. on Modeling and Simulation* (Pittsburgh, PA, 1980), pp. 135–139.

RANJ80c   S. E. Ranjbaran and R. J. Swallow, "Computer Graphics of Complex Images in Training," in *Proc. of Workshop on Picture Data Description and Management* (Pacific Grove, CA, August 27–28, 1980), pp. 207–212.

REEV81   W. T. Reeves, "Inbetweening for Computer Animation Utilizing Moving Point Constraints," *Comput. Graphics*, **15**(3), pp. 263–269 (August 1981).

RHEN80   J. Rhen, "Military Simulators—Total Training," *Nat. Defense*, pp. 32–35, 64, 66 (February 1980). (Describes a ship simulator built by Sperry Rand using an E&S visual system.)

ROMN68   G. W. Romney, G. S. Watkins, and D. C. Evans, "Real-Time Display of Computer Generated Half-Tone Pictures," *Proc. IFIP Cong.*, 1968, pp. 973–978.

ROSC71   S. N. Roscoe, "Incremental Transfer Effectiveness," *Human Factors*, **14**, pp. 363–364 (1971).

ROUG68   R. S. Rougelot, "Digitally Computed Images for Visual Simulation," in *Proc. 3rd Naval Training Center and Industry Conf.* (Orlando, FL, November 19–21, 1968), pp. 38–44.

ROUG69   R. S. Rougelot, "The General Electric Computed Color TV Display," in *Pertinent Concepts in Computer Graphics*, M. Faiman and J. Nieverselt, Eds., University of Illinois Press, 1969, pp. 261–268.

ROWL80   T. Rowley, "Computer Generated Images for Training Simulators," in *Proc. 1980 ONLINE Computer Graphic Conf.* (Brighton, England, August 1980), ONLINE Publ., Northwood Hills, Middlesex, England, 1980, pp. 223–232.

SCHA78   B. J. Schachter, "Decomposition of Polygons into Convex Sets," *IEEE Trans. Comput.*, **C-72**(11), pp. 1078–1082 (November 1978).

SCHA80a   B. J. Schachter, "Long Crested Wave Models," *Comput. Graphics and Image Process* , **12**, pp. 187–201 (1980). (Describes a statistical model for real-time texture generation.)

SCHA80b   B. J. Schachter and N. Ahuja, "A History of Visual Flight Simulation," *Comput. Graphics World*, **3**(3), pp. 16–31 (May 1980).

SCHA80c   B. J. Schachter, "Real Time Display of Texture," in *Proc. 5th Int. Conf. on Pattern Recognition* (Miami, FL, December 1980), pp. 789–791.

SCHA81   B. J. Schachter, "Computer Image Generation for Flight Simulation," *IEEE Comput. Graphics and Appl.*, **1**(4), pp. 29–68 (October 1981).

SCHN76   A. P. Schnitzer, "A Data Base for Digital Image Generation," in *Proc. 9th Naval Training Equipment Conf.* (Orlando, FL, November 1976), pp. 103–113.

SCHU69   R. A. Schumacker, B. Brand, M. Gilliland, and W. Sharp, "Study for Applying Computer Generated Images to Simulation," AFHRL-TR-69-14, Air Force Human Resources Lab., Wright-Patterson AFB, OH, September 1969.

SCHU71   R. A. Schumacker and R. S. Rougelot, "Low Visibility Effects for Computer Generated Systems," *1971 Int. Symp. on Information Display*, Lewis Winner, New York, 1971.

SCHU77   R. A. Schumacker and R. S. Rougelot, "Image Quality—A Comparison of Night/Dusk and Day/Night CGI Systems," *ICAO Bull.*, pp. 17–21 (April 1978). (Also in *Proc. 1977 Image Conf.*, Air Force Human Resource Lab., Williams AFB, AZ.)

SCHU80   R. A. Schumacker, "A New Visual System Architecture," in *Proc. 2nd Interservice/Industry Training Equipment Conf.* (Salt Lake City, UT, November 18–20, 1980), pp. 94–101. (Describes E&S CT-5.)

SEMP79   C. A. Semple, R. T. Hennessy, M. S. Sanders, B. K. Cross, and B. H. Beith, *Simulator Training Requirements and Efficiency Study*, Canyon Research Group, West Lake Village, CA, October 1979.

SHIN74   B. J. Shinn, "Computer Generated T.V. Imagery," *SID J.*, **11**(5), pp. 6–9 (September/October 1974).

SHOH70   M. Shohat, "Esoteric Simulator Pact to Hughes—The F-18 Weapons Tactics Trainer," *Mil. Electron./Countermeasures*, pp. 80–91 (November 1979).

SINO80   H. J. Sinofsky, "COMPUTROL: Computer Color/Halftone Image Generation through Hardware/Software," in *Proc. 11th Annual Pittsburgh Conf. on Modeling and Simulation* (Pittsburgh, PA, 1980), pp. 147–153. (As good a discussion of their system as is available.)

SMIT79   A. R. Smith, "Tint Fill," *Comput. Graphics*, **13**(2), pp. 276–283 (August 1979).

SOLA81   D. Soland, M. Voth, and P. Narendra, "Real-Time Feasibility for Generation of Nonlinear Textured Terrain," TR-79-27, for Air Force Human Resource Lab., Air Force Systems Command, Brooks AFB, TX, by Honeywell Co., January 1981.

SPOO75   A. M. Spooner, "Collimated Displays for Flight Simulation," in *SPIE*, vol. 59: *Simulators and Simulation*, 1975, pp. 108–113.

SPOO77   A. M. Spooner, "Visual Flight Simulation Experiencing Continual Improvement," *ICAO Bull.*, pp. 18–21 (1977). (Describes an E&S calligraphic system.)

SPOO80   A. M. Spooner, D. R. Breglia, and B. W. Patz, "Realscan—A CIG System with Increased Image Detail," in *Proc. 2nd Interservice/Industry Training Equipment Conf.* (Salt Lake City, UT, November 18–20, 1980), pp. 110–116.

SPRO68   R. F. Sproull and I. E. Sutherland, "A Clipping Divider," *AFIPS FJCC Proc.*, vol. 33, 1968, pp. 765–775.

STAP78   K. T. Staple, "Technical Evaluation Report of the Specialists' Meeting of the Flight Mechanics Panel on Piloted Aircraft Environment Simulation Technology," AGARD-AR-126, NATO Advisory Group for Aerospace Research and Development, Neuilly-sur-Seine, France, 1978.

STEI79   K. J. Stein, "Image Systems Developed for New Flight Simulators," *Aviat. Week and Space Technol.*, pp. 181–182 (March 12, 1979).

STEI80   K. J. Stein, "GE Sets Simulation Goals," *Aviat. Week and Space Technol.*, pp. 105–109 (February 11, 1980).

STRA78   T. M. Strat, "Application of Data Flow Computation to the Shaded Image Problem," Working Paper 167, MIT Artificial Intelligence Lab., Cambridge, MA, May 1978.

SUTH70   I. E. Sutherland, "Computer Displays," *Sci. Am.*, **222**(6), pp. 36–41 (June 1970).

SUTH73a   I. E. Sutherland, "Polygon Sorting by Subdivision: A Solution to the Hidden Surface Problem." Unpublished (1973).

SUTH73b   I. E. Sutherland, R. F. Sproull, and R. A. Schumacker, "Sorting and the Hidden Surface Problem," in *Proc. AFIPS 1973 National Computer Cong.*, vol. 42, 1973, pp. 685–693.

SUTH74a   I. E. Sutherland, R. F. Sproull, and R. A. Schumacker, "A Characterization of Ten Hidden Surface Algorithms," *ACM Comput. Surv.*, **6**(1), pp. 1–55 (May 1974). (A landmark paper.)

SUTH74b   I. E. Sutherland and G. W. Hodgman, "Reentrant Polygon Clipping," *Commun. ACM*, **17**(1), pp. 32–42 (January 1974). (Another landmark paper.)

SWAL74   R. J. Swallow, "CHARGE Interactive Graphics System Terminal: Theory of Operation," TR 74-26, Human Resources Research Org., Alexandria, VA, December 1974.

SWAL78   R. J. Swallow, R. Goodwin, and R. Draudin, "COMPUTROL: A New Approach to Computer Generated Imagery," in SPIE, vol. 162: *Visual Simulation and Image Realism*, 1978, pp. 16–25.

SZAB78   N. S. Szabo, "Digital Image Anomalies: Static and Dynamic," in SPIE, vol. 162: *Visual Simulation and Realism*, August 30, 1978, pp. 11–15.

THOR78   J. A. Thorpe, N. C. Varneg, R. W. McFadden, W. D. LeMaster, and L. H. Short, "Training Effectiveness of Three Types of Visual Systems for KC-135 Flight Simulators," AFHRL-TR-78-16, Air Force Human Resource Lab., Williams AFB, AZ, June 1978.

VORS76   C. J. Vorst, "A New Visual Simulation Technique for Pilot Training," in *Proc. 9th Naval Training Equipment Conf.* (Orlando, FL, November 1976), pp. 115–125. (The best description of Gould's system.)

WADE79   J. Wadell, "A Look at the New 747 Simulator," *Boeing Airliner*, pp. 3–5 (October 1979).

WARN69   J. Warnock, "A Hidden-Surface Algorithm for Computer Generated Half-Tone Pictures," University of Utah, Computer Science Dept., TR 4-15, 1969.

WATK70   G. S. Watkins, "A Real Time Visible Surface Algorithm," Doctoral Dissertation, TR 70-101, University of Utah, Computer Science Dept., June 1970.

WEIN78   R. Weinberg, "Computer Graphics in Support of Space Shuttle Simulation," *ACM Comput. Graphics*, **12,** pp. 82–86, (1978). Also in *Comput. Graphics World*, **12**(3), pp. 25–28 (March/April 1979).

WEIN82   R. Weinberg, "An Architecture for Parallel Processing Image Synthesis with Anti-Aliasing," Ph.D. Thesis, University of Minnesota, February 8, 1982.

WILD71   E. C. Wild, R. S. Rougelot, and R. A. Schumacker, "Computing Full Color Perspective Images," Rep. R71ELS-26, General Electric Co., Electronics Lab., Syracuse, NY, May 1971.

WOHL80   M. R. Wohlers, S. Hsiao, J. Mendelsohn, and G. Y. Gardner, "Computer Simulation of Synthetic Aperture Radar Images of Three-Dimensional Objects," *IEEE Trans. Aerosp. Electron. Sys.*, **16**(3), pp. 258–271 (May 1980).

WOOD79   S. Woodcock and J. D. Leyland, "High Resolution CRTs and Their Application to Helmet-Mounted Displays," in *Proc. SPIE*, vol. 20, no. 2, Second Quarter, 1979.

WOON70   P. Woon, "A Computer Procedure for Generating Visible-Line Drawings of Solids Bounded by Quadric Surfaces," Tech. Rep. 403-15, New York University, Dept. of Electrical Engineering, December 1970.

YAMA75   M. Yamamoto and T. Taneda, "Laser Displays," in *Advances in Image Pickup and Display*, B. Kazan, Ed., Academic Press, New York, 1975, pp. 1–58.

YAN79   J. K. Yan, "Real Time Generation and Smooth Shading of Quadric Surfaces," in *Proc. 1st Interservice/Industry Training Equipment Conf.* (Orlando, FL, November 1979), pp. 247–260.

YAN80   J. K. Yan, "Computer Generation of Curvilinear Objects," in *Proc. 2nd Interservice/Industry Training Equipment Conf.* (Salt Lake City, UT, November 18–20, 1980), pp. 37–45.

AUTHOR INDEX

SUBJECT INDEX